INTERNATIONAL RELATIONS: THE ERA OF THE COLD WAR 1943–1991

GCSE Modern World History for Edexcel

Steve Waugh
John Wright
REVISED BY CHRIS CULPIN

HODDER
EDUCATION
AN HACHETTE UK COMPANY

For Gary Bowler, Mick Wright and the 79ers. A very special group.

In order to ensure that this resource offers high quality support for the associated Edexcel qualification, it has been through a review process by the awarding body to confirm that it fully covers the teaching and learning content of the specification or part of a specification at which it is aimed, and demonstrates an appropriate balance between the development of subject skills, knowledge and understanding, in addition to preparation for assessment.

While the publishers have made every attempt to ensure that advice on the qualification and its assessment is accurate, the official specification and associated assessment guidance materials are the only authoritative source of information and should always be referred to for definitive guidance.

Edexcel examiners have not contributed to any sections in this resource relevant to examination papers for which they have responsibility.

No material from an endorsed resource will be used verbatim in any assessment set by Edexcel.

Endorsement of a resource does not mean that the resource is required to achieve this Edexcel qualification, nor does it mean that it is the only suitable material available to support the qualification, and any resource lists produced by the awarding body shall include this and other appropriate resources.

The Publishers would like to thank the following for permission to reproduce copyright material:

Photo credits

p. 6 © Bettmann/ CORBIS; p. 9 © Punch; p. 10 © David King Collection; p. 11 © Bettmann/ CORBIS; p. 12 © Bettmann/ CORBIS; p. 14 © Hulton-Deutsch Collection/ CORBIS; p. 16 © Hulton-Deutsch Collection/ CORBIS; p. 18 © Punch; p. 19 © David King Collection; p. 21 L.G. Illingworth, National Library of Wales, Aberystwyth © Solo Syndication; p. 23 © Punch; p. 24 © Jim Pringle/ Empics/ AP; p. 25 © Peter Newark; p. 26 © White-Thomson Publishing; p. 28 © Punch; p. 30 *tl* © David King Collection; p. 30 *bl* © Punch; p. 30 *r* © Bettmann/ CORBIS; p. 31 © Punch; p. 33 © Keystone/ Getty Images; p. 36 © Punch; p. 37 © AKG/ Ullstein Bild; p. 39 © David King Collection; p. 43 © AP/ Empics; p. 45 © Erich Lessing/ Magnum; p. 46 *ml* © Bettmann/ CORBIS; p. 46 *bl* © John Frost Historical Newspapers; p. 49 *l* © Bettmann/ CORBIS; p. 49 *r* © Paul Schutzer/ Time-Life Pictures/ Getty Images; p. 51 © Bettmann/ CORBIS; p. 52 © Popperfoto; p. 53 © Bettmann/ CORBIS; p. 54 *r* © Camera Press; p. 57 © Punch Limited/ Topfoto; p. 58 © MIGUEL VINAS/ AFP/ Getty Images; p. 61 © AFP/ Getty Images; p. 62 © Leslie Illingworth/ University of Kent; p. 65 *l* © Hulton-Deutsch Collection/ CORBIS; p. 65 *r* © Libor Hajsky/ EPA/ CORBIS; p. 66 © Bettmann/ CORBIS; p. 67 © Miroslav Zajíc/ CORBIS; p. 68 © Alain Nogues/ CORBIS SYGMA; p. 70 © EPA/ CORBIS; p. 71 *t* © Bettmann/ CORBIS; p. 71 *b* © MIROSLAV ZAJÍC/ CORBIS; p. 76 © AP/ Empics; p. 77 © AFP/ Getty Images; p. 78 © Bettman/ CORBIS; p. 79 © Time-Life Pictures/ US Air Force/ Getty Images; p. 80 © Les Gibbard/ Guardian Archive; p. 81 *t* © Bettmann/ CORBIS; p. 81 *b* © Popperfoto; p. 82 © AP/ Empics; p. 85 © el Lipchitz/ AP Photo/ Empics; p. 88 © Grace/ Keystone USA/ Rex Features; p. 89 © Les Gibbard/ Guardian Archive; p. 90 © Rex Features; p. 93 *l* © Arthur Grace/ Rex Features; p. 93 *r* © Sipa Press/ Rex Features; p. 94 *tl* © Bettmann/ CORBIS; p. 94 *r* © Nils Jorgensen/ Rex Features; p. 97 © Corbis; p. 99 © RIA Novosti Photo Library; p. 100 © Peter Heimsath/ Rex Features; p. 101 © Reuters/ CORBIS; p. 102 *l* © RIA Novosti Photo Library; p. 102 *r* © Peter Turnley/ CORBIS; p. 104 © Chris Niedenthal/ Time-Life Pictures/ Getty Images; p. 105 © David Brauchli/ Reuters/ CORBIS.

Acknowledgements

p. 5 Edexcel Limited; p. 7 and 29 C. Culpin, *Making History*, Collins, 1984; p. 10, 28 and 46 S. Waugh, *Essential Modern World History*, Nelson Thornes, 2001; p. 11 *ml* D. Phillips, *Hitler and the Rise of the Nazis*, Hill and Fell, 1968; p. 11 *tl* A. White, *Russia and USSR*, Collins, 1994; p. 15 *mr*, p. 15 *tl*, p. 15 *tr*, p. 16, p. 37 *tr*, p. 41 *l* and *r*, p. 67 *l*, p. 67 *r* and p. 72 B. Walsh, *Modern World History*, J. Murray, 2001; p. 29 *tr* C. Culpin, *Making History*, Collins, 1984; p. 17, 21 and 23 J. Aylett, *The Cold War and After*, Hodder, 1996;
p. 18 J. Isaacs and T. Downing, *Cold War: An Illustrated History, 1945–1991*, Bantam Press 1998; p. 19 from George Kennan, "The Sources of Soviet Conduct" (1947), reprinted at www.historyguide.org/europe/kennan.html; p. 26 *l* from a report to Cominform by Andrei Zhdanov, reproduced at www.cnn.com/SPECIALS/cold.war/episodes/04/documents/cominform.html; p. 26 *r* from "The Rise of Comecon", *Time* magazine, 4 July 1960; p. 27 *b*, 27 *t*, 29 *mr*, 36 and 37 *bl* T. Lancaster and D. Peaple, *The Modern World* Causeway, 2000; p. 33 from a facsimile at www.learningcurve.gov.uk/coldwar/G4/cs1/s4.htm; p. 39 from the North Atlantic Treaty Organisation charter, 4 April 1949; p. 44 *bl*, 45, 81, 85 *mr*, 85 *tr* and 86 *tr* P. Fisher, *The Great Power Conflict*, Blackwell, 1985; p. 44 *br* P. Shuter, *Skills in History*, Heinemann, 1988; p. 48 L. Hartley, *Superpower Relations Since 1945*, Bell and Hyman, 1988; p. 51 *bl*, 51 *tl*, 51 *mr*, 53 *l*, 63, 98 *ml* and 104 *l* T. McAleavy, *Modern World History*, CUP, 1996; p. 51 *ml* W. Taubman, *Khrushchev*, Free Press, 2005; p. 53 *r* from 'American Experience' – The Presidents, on www.pbs.org; p. 56 B. Walsh and W. Birks, *Revision for History: GCSE Modern World History*, J. Murray, 1996; p. 59 Richard J. Walton, *Cold War and Counter-Revolution: The Foreign Policy of John F. Kennedy*, 1972; p. 60, 62 *l*, 75, 82, 88 *l* and 91 J. Fitzgerald, *Soviet-American Relations in the Nuclear Age*, Nelson, 1988; p. 62 *r* P. Shuter, *Skills in History*, Heinemann, 1988; p. 69 and 70 *ml* P. Sauvain, *Key Themes of the Twentieth Century* Nelson Thornes, 1996; p. 80 S. Judges, *Superpower Rivalry*, Longman, 1994; p. 84 J. Laver, *Stagnation and Reform*, Hodder, 1997; p. 99 T. Downey and Nigel Smith, *Russia and the USSR*, OUP, 1996; p. 100 M. Gorbachev, *Memoirs*, Doubleday Inc., 1996; p. 104 *r* adapted from a narration of the event under 'The Sinatra Doctrine' on www.wikipedia.org; p. 106 adapted from the presentation speech of the 1990 Nobel Peace Prize, given by Gidske Anderson, Chairperson of the Norwegian Nobel Committee, to Mikhail Gorbachev.

Every effort has been made to trace all copyright holders, but if any have been inadvertently overlooked the Publishers will be pleased to make the necessary arrangements at the first opportunity.

Although every effort has been made to ensure that website addresses are correct at time of going to press, Hodder Education cannot be held responsible for the content of any website mentioned in this book. It is sometimes possible to find a relocated web page by typing in the address of the home page for a website in the URL window of your browser.

Orders: please contact Bookpoint Ltd, 130 Milton Park, Abingdon, Oxon OX14 4SB. Telephone: (44) 01235 827720. Fax: (44) 01235 400454. Lines are open 9.00 – 5.00, Monday to Saturday, with a 24-hour message answering service. Visit our website at www.hoddereducation.co.uk.

© John Wright, Steve Waugh 2006, 2009
First published in 2006 by
Hodder Education,
An Hachette UK Company
338 Euston Road
London NW1 3BH

This second edition published 2009

Impression number   8
Year   2014

Cover photos © Bettmann/CORBIS – Mikhail Gorbachev and Ronald Reagan; © Bettmann/CORBIS – Marines with machine gun.
Typeset in Adobe Garamond 12 pt by White-Thomson Publishing Ltd
Printed in Dubai

A catalogue record for this title is available from the British Library.

ISBN: 978 0340 984 390

Contents

Introduction

About the course

During this course you must study four units:

- **Unit 1** International Relations: The era of the Cold War 1943–1991
- **Unit 2** Modern World Depth Study
- **Unit 3** Modern World Source Enquiry
- **Unit 4** Representations of History.

These units are assessed through three examination papers and one controlled assessment:

- In Paper 1 you have one hour and 15 minutes to answer six questions on Unit 1.
- In Paper 2 you have one hour and 15 minutes to answer six questions on Unit 2.
- In Paper 3 you have one hour and 15 minutes to answer five questions on Unit 3.
- In the controlled assessment you have to complete a task under controlled conditions in the classroom (Unit 4).

International relations (Paper 1)

There are three key topics in the International Relations unit. Each key topic covers a different period. You have to study all three key topics. These are:

- **Key Topic 1** How did the Cold War in Europe develop? 1943–56
- **Key Topic 2** Three Cold War crises: Berlin, Cuba and Czechoslovakia c1957–69
- **Key Topic 3** Why did the Cold War end? From *détente* (1972) to the collapse of the Soviet Union (1991).

About the book

The book is divided into the three key topics. Each key topic is then divided into chapters which give you the key information you need in order to make judgements on the following issues:

- Why the USA and Soviet Union, allies during the Second World War, became fierce rivals in 1945.
- Why the USA and Britain were forced to airlift supplies into West Berlin, 1948–49, and what impact events in Berlin had on the development of the Cold War.
- The impact of Soviet rule on Hungary and how two rival alliance systems, NATO and the Warsaw Pact, emerged.
- Why the Berlin Wall was built.
- Why the crisis in Cuba brought the world to the brink of war.
- Why Soviet tanks were sent into countries such as Hungary and Czechoslovakia to put down uprisings.
- Why the Soviet invasion of Afghanistan led to the collapse of *détente.*
- How the Superpowers became involved in an arms race, creating weapons of mass destruction capable of destroying the world.
- Why the Cold War came to a sudden end in 1990.

Each chapter in this book:
- Contains activities – some develop the historical skills you will need, others give you the opportunity to practise exam skills.
- Gives step-by-step guidance, model answers and advice on how to answer particular question types in Paper 1.
- Defines key terms and highlights glossary terms in bold the first time they appear in each section.

About Paper 1

Paper 1 is a test of your ability to remember important information about all the topics in this Unit. You will have to select from what you remember in order to show your knowledge and understanding in answer to brief questions, extended essay questions and questions to test your understanding of historical sources and how they are used.

Below is a set of specimen questions (without the sources). You will be given step-by-step guidance throughout the book on how best to approach and answer these type of questions.

Question 1 is a brief 2-mark question in which you have to read a source and find two points from it.

Question 2 requires a slightly longer answer than question 1. You have to make two statements which answer the question and add some detail to each from your own knowledge.

Question 3 requires some planning. You have to analyse the value and limitations of two sources from the point of view of their content and reliability. Having done that, you have to make a judgement about how useful each one is for a particular enquiry.

In the exam, you would have a choice of two questions here, 4(a) and 4(b). Having chosen one, you need to write at least two statements about the topic, strengthening each one with additional detail, explaining why it is a 'key feature'.

EXAM

PAPER 1

1 Give **two** reasons from Source A why relations between the Allies continued to worsen at the time of the Potsdam Conference. (Source A, line 1)

(2 marks)

2 Outline **two** issues on which the Allies agreed at the Potsdam Conference.

(4 marks)

3 How useful are Sources B and C as evidence of the purpose of the Marshall Plan? Explain your answer, using Sources B and C and your own knowledge.

(10 marks)

4 Describe the key features of the Cuban Missiles Crisis.

(6 marks)

5 Explain the importance of three of the following in the Cold War:
   The Berlin Airlift, 1948–49
   • The Warsaw Pact, 1955
   • The Prague Spring, 1968
   • The Helsinki Agreements, 1975

(15 marks)

6 Explain why relations between the USA and the Soviet Union changed in the years 1980–1985.   (13 marks)
   You may use the following in your answer:
   • The Soviet invasion of Afghanistan
   • The election of Ronald Reagan as President of the USA
   You must also include information of your own.
   (Total for spelling, punctuation and grammar = 3 marks)
   (Total for question 6 = 16 marks)

In Question 5 you are given four events which could come from anywhere in the unit and which relate to one of its big issues. You have to choose three, describe each one in some detail and explain why it is important in the history of that issue.

Question 6 is an essay question which asks you to explain reasons for a change. You need to explain at least three reasons in detail, showing how they linked together and which was the most important. The accuracy of your spelling, punctuation and grammar is also assessed in this question (3 of the marks are allocated to this).

An American and Soviet soldier shake hands in 1945 at the River Elbe, where the two allied armies met at the end of the Second World War.

Task

What impression of relations between the USA and the Soviet Union do you get from this photograph?

This key topic examines the key developments in international relations from the Teheran Conference of 1943, through the beginning of the Cold War, to the Hungarian Crisis of 1956.

This was a period of great change in the relations between the two Superpowers – from being allies during the Second World War, to the build-up of rivalry and tension from as early as 1948–49 in the Berlin Crisis. By 1956 the USA and Soviet Union had formed two rival alliance systems and were competing with each other in **nuclear weapons** development and the space race.

Each chapter within this section explains a key issue and examines important lines of enquiry as outlined below.

Chapter 1 The origins of the Cold War (pages 7–20)

- What was meant by the 'Cold War' and 'Superpowers'?
- To what extent was there rivalry before 1945?
- Why was there a widening gulf between the allies during the the peace conferences of 1945?

Chapter 2 The early Cold War 1945–47 (pages 21–32)

- How and why did the Soviet Union control Eastern Europe?
- What was meant by the 'iron curtain'?
- How did the Cold War intensify in the years 1945–47?

Chapter 3 The Berlin Crisis and its aftermath (pages 33–40)

- Why was the Berlin Crisis of 1948–49 a significant event?
- Why were NATO and the Warsaw Pact important in the Cold War?
- How and why did an arms race develop in these years?

Chapter 4 The Hungarian uprising (pages 41–47)

- Why did the Hungarian uprising take place?
- What were the key features of the uprising?
- What were the results of the uprising?

The origins of the Cold War

Source A: Joseph Stalin speaking in 1945 about Churchill, the British Prime Minister, and Roosevelt, the US President, who were his allies

Perhaps you think that, because we are allies of the English, we have forgotten who they are and who Churchill is. They find nothing sweeter than to trick their allies. And Churchill? Churchill is the kind who, if you don't watch him, will slip a kopek out of your pocket. And Roosevelt? Roosevelt is not like that. He dips his hand only for bigger coins.

Task

Read Source A. Do you get the impression that Stalin trusted his allies?

The alliance between the USA, Britain and the Soviet Union during the Second World War (1939–45) was very much a marriage of convenience or necessity, the necessity being to defeat Nazi Germany. Once Germany had been defeated, differences began to emerge between Stalin and the Soviet Union on one side, who wanted security against future invasion by controlling eastern Europe, and the USA and Britain on the other, who feared the spread of Soviet **communism** to western Europe.

This chapter will answer the following questions:

*   What was meant by the 'Cold War' and 'Superpowers'?
*   To what extent was there Superpower rivalry before 1945?
*   Why did the peace conferences of 1945 intensify this rivalry?
*   Who was to blame for the Cold War?

Exam skills

This chapter gives guidance on the first question on Paper 1. This question, which is worth 2 marks, asks you to read and understand a source and extract two pieces of information from it.

What was meant by the 'Cold War' and 'Superpowers'?

What was the Cold War?

A hot war is a conflict in which actual fighting takes place. A cold war is a war waged against an enemy by every means short of actually fighting. The expression was first used to describe the frosty atmosphere that developed between the Superpowers in the years following the end of the Second World War.

The Cold War started in 1945–46 and lasted for over 40 years. At first it was confined to Europe, but during the 1950s and 1960s it spread into Asia and then worldwide as the Superpowers competed for influence or control over newly independent states, especially in Africa.

Indeed the Cold War had nearly all the features of a hot war:

- It had causes and consequences.
- There were two sides – East v. West or the USA and its supporters v. the Soviet Union and its supporters.
- There were two rival armed camps – NATO v. Warsaw Pact (see pages 39–40)
- The two sides competed for influence all over the world, often assisting rival sides in **civil wars** such as the conflicts in Korea (1950–53) and Vietnam (1960s).

However, the two Superpowers did not ever directly fight each other.

What were its main features?

Spying	Both sides spied on each other. This was mainly to find out any military developments. They even used spy planes which could fly at a great height and take photographs. One example was the American U2 spy plane which could fly high enough to avoid being shot down by Soviet fighters. Spying increased the rivalry between the two sides.
Propaganda	Both sides used propaganda to create the worst possible image of the other side and ensure that national public opinion supported the government. The Soviet Union even used success in sport, especially the Olympics, to illustrate the superiority of the communist system.
Arms race	There was competition in **conventional** as well as nuclear weapons. Each side wanted more weapons and newer technology than the other. By the 1960s, both sides had enough nuclear weapons to destroy each other many times over. This was called 'Mutually Assured Destruction' or **MAD** theory. In reality this acted as a deterrent against war, although it did not stop each side from trying to develop even more advanced nuclear weapons.
Space race	Each side competed for success in the space race. At first it was to launch the first satellite, then the first man in space and finally the first man on the Moon. Success in this field again was very effective propaganda for both the USA and the Soviet Union.
Loans and aid	Each side competed to provide loans and aid to less developed and often newly independent states in order to win their support in the Cold War.

Source A: A British cartoon from *Punch* magazine showing the Soviet Union represented by the bear

Who were the Superpowers?

Before the Second World War there were several 'Great Powers' including Britain, France, Germany, the USA, Japan and the Soviet Union. The Second World War changed this situation:

- Germany and Japan were defeated and seriously weakened.
- France had been defeated and occupied by Germany during the war and lost its status as a great power.
- Britain was victorious but almost bankrupt.

Two countries, however, emerged even stronger and were clearly far more economically and militarily powerful than the rest of the world. These were the USA and the Soviet Union.

Tasks

1. Draw a diagram to show the differences between a hot war and a cold war.

2. a) What do you think the bear is doing in the cartoon (Source A)?

   b) What message is the cartoonist trying to get across?

3. a) Which of the four factors in the table below do you think is the most important in determining Superpower status? Explain your answer.

   b) How are the four factors linked?

FACTORS	USA	SOVIET UNION
Geographical size (1980s)	Nine million sq. acres	21 million sq. acres
Population (1980s)	226 million	226 million
Nuclear weapons (1980s)	2 million	4.8 million
Economy (1984)	$ 2100 million GNP	$ 1200 million GNP

To what extent was there Superpower rivalry before 1945?

Rivalry before 1941

Superpower rivalry was not new. The differences and rivalry go back to the **Bolshevik** or communist revolution in Russia in 1917. The Bolsheviks, led by Lenin, seized control of the government and over the next few years established a communist government. They believed in world revolution. So, at the heart of the rivalry were the conflicting ideas of the two sides – communism and capitalism.

	Communism	Capitalism
Politics	Only one political party – the Communist Party. No choice. Unable to change their government.	Several parties – voters may choose and change their government.
Economy	No private industry or businesses. No private profit. All industry and businesses owned by the state for the benefit of everyone.	Most industry and businesses privately owned.
Beliefs	Everyone equal. Belief in world revolution, that is, encouraging communism in other countries. Censorship of the media.	Some will be wealthier than others. Spread influence to other countries to encourage trade and investment. Very little censorship of media.

The differences between communism and capitalism

Countries such as Britain, France and the USA, who believed in capitalism, feared the spread of communism. They intervened in the Russian Civil War, 1918–21, giving arms and supplies to the groups in Russia who were fighting to overthrow Lenin and the communists. Despite their victory in the civil war, Lenin and other leading Bolsheviks were very suspicious of the West. Differences between Bolshevik Russia and the West can be seen in the following sources.

> **Source A: From a speech by Lenin in 1919**
>
> *England, America and France are waging war against Russia. They are avenging themselves on the Soviet Union for having overthrown the landlords and capitalists. They are helping the landlords with money and supplies.*

> **Source B: A Bolshevik propaganda poster. The three figures represent France, the USA and Britain**

Source C: **From a speech by Winston Churchill, 1919, who was a member of the British government**

Of all the tyrannies in history, the Bolshevik tyranny is the worst, the most destructive and the most degrading. Lenin and his government are committing the worst atrocities possible.

Such differences intensified in the years after 1933 when Hitler became leader of Germany. Hitler, who hated communism, wanted to expand eastwards and destroy the Soviet Union.

Source D: **From a speech by Hitler in 1933**

If a single people in Western or Central Europe were to succumb to Bolshevism, this poison would spread farther and would destroy that which is today the oldest and fairest cultural treasure in the world. By taking upon herself this struggle against Bolshevism, Germany is fulfilling a European mission.

Stalin, who became leader of the Soviet Union in 1928 after Lenin's death, was especially fearful of an invasion from the West. Indeed he was convinced that Britain, France and the USA would ally with Nazi Germany in the 1930s and encourage Hitler to invade.

Britain, France and the USA disliked Stalin even more when he signed an alliance with Hitler in 1939 known as the Nazi-Soviet Pact. They feared, rightly, that Stalin wanted to seize part of neighbouring Poland.

Source E: **An American cartoon from October 1939 about the Nazi-Soviet Pact. Hitler is shown on the left and Stalin on the right.**

WONDER HOW LONG THE HONEYMOON WILL LAST?

Tasks

1. a) What message is the cartoonist trying to put across in Source B?

   b) How does the cartoonist get across this message?

2. Describe the key features of Superpower rivalry before 1945.

3. Does Source C support the evidence of Source A about the Bolsheviks and their aims?

4. What can you learn from Source D about Hitler's attitude towards Bolshevism?

5. What is the purpose of Source E?

6. Odd one out:
   • Identify the odd word out in the following:

      communism   one-party   private industry

   • Explain your choice.
   • Add a word that replaces the odd one out and links with the other two.
   • Put together your own example of 'odd one out' based on Superpower rivalry before 1945.
   • Try it out on someone in your class.

Rivalry during the Second World War

The Soviet Union allied with Britain and the USA during the Second World War in what became known as the Grand Alliance. Stalin was forced into this arrangement by the German invasion of the Soviet Union in June 1941. During the war the Grand Alliance held two conferences. The first meeting of the Big Three – President Franklin Roosevelt of the USA, Prime Minister Winston Churchill of Great Britain and Stalin – was held in Tehran, the capital of Iran, in 1943. The second was in Yalta, a Soviet resort on the Black Sea, in 1945 (see page 14).

The Teheran Conference

Roosevelt was keen to improve relations between the three Allies and agreed to hold the meeting in Teheran, Iran, near to the Soviet Union in November 1943.

The meeting was mainly a success for Stalin who achieved most of what he wanted. This was because Roosevelt was not well during the Conference and, in any case, tended to side with Stalin rather than Churchill. For example, Churchill's idea of an Allied invasion through the Balkans, thereby preventing the Red Army from taking over all of Eastern Europe, was rejected. The main agreements were:

- Britain and the USA agreed to open up a second front by invading France in May 1944.

- The Soviet Union was to wage war against Japan once Germany was defeated.

- A **United Nations** organisation was to be set up after the war.

- An area of eastern Poland was added to the Soviet Union. At the insistence of Stalin, the borders of post-war Poland were to be along the Oder and Neisse rivers (see map on page 22).

Strains in the Grand Alliance

Second Front
Stalin was annoyed that Britain and the USA delayed opening a second front (they did so only in 1944 with the D-Day landings). Stalin was convinced that the British and Americans were waiting until the Soviet Union had been seriously damaged by the German invaders.

Churchill
Winston Churchill had been a staunch opponent of the Bolshevik Revolution. As secretary of state for war, he had supported the Bolsheviks' enemies in the Civil War of 1918–21 (see page 10). As British prime minister during the Second World War, he was suspicious of Stalin's motives in eastern Europe. He was convinced that Soviet troops would remain in countries they liberated from the Germans.

Poland
Britain had gone to war in September 1939 to maintain the independence of Poland. However, Stalin believed that Soviet control of Poland was essential to prevent future invasions. Churchill became even more suspicious of Stalin's motives in Poland when, in April 1943, German troops discovered a mass grave in the Katyn Forest near Smolensk. This grave contained the bodies of 10,000 Polish officers murdered by the Soviets in 1939.

Warsaw Uprising
In August 1944 the Polish resistance organised an uprising in Warsaw against the German forces occupying the city. The Soviet army, which had reached the outskirts of the city, halted its advance and stood by as the uprising was brutally crushed by the Germans. This defeat left the Poles defenceless against a Soviet occupation.

The Big Three (from left to right, Stalin, Roosevelt and Churchill) at the Teheran Conference, 1943.

Tasks

1. *Describe one way in which relations among the members of the Grand Alliance became strained during the years 1942–45.*

2. *In what ways did the Teheran Conference:*
   - *strengthen the Grand Alliance*
   - *weaken the Grand Alliance?*

Why did the peace conferences of 1945 intensify this rivalry?

Look at the two photographs of the allied leaders on these pages and on pages 16–17. What changes have taken place between the two conferences? These changes were to have profound effects on relations between the Superpowers.

The Yalta Conference, February 1945

By early 1945 Allied armies were closing in on Berlin, and Germany was close to defeat. The three Allied leaders met at Yalta in early 1945 to consider what to do with Germany and Europe once victory was achieved. The Big Three were still fearful of Hitler and, for the most part, were able to reach agreement on key issues.

Yet this was the last meeting of the Big Three. Within months, Roosevelt had died and Churchill had lost a general election. Stalin wanted the Germans to pay huge reparations, but Roosevelt and Churchill agreed that it was not sensible to punish Germany too harshly. Stalin and Roosevelt apparently enjoyed a warm relationship, and as a result, Churchill felt isolated for most of the Conference.

They agreed:

- The Soviet Union would enter the war against Japan once Germany had surrendered.
- To divide Germany into four zones: US, British, French and Soviet.
- To divide Berlin into four zones in the same way.
- To hunt down and try Nazi war criminals in an international court of justice.
- To allow countries that had been liberated from occupation by the German army to have free elections to choose the government they wanted.
- To join the new United Nations Organisation in order to maintain peace once the war ended.
- That eastern Europe would be a Soviet 'sphere of influence'.

Churchill, Roosevelt and Stalin (left to right) at the peace conference at Yalta, February 1945

Source A: Stalin, proposing a toast at a dinner at the Yalta Conference, 1945

I want to drink to our alliance, that it should not lose its intimacy, its free expression of views. I know of no such close alliance of three Great Powers as this. May it be strong and stable, may we be as frank as possible.

Source B: Milovan Djilas, vice-president of Yugoslavia, writing about Yalta in 1948

In the hallway of Yalta we stopped before a map of the world on which the Soviet Union was coloured in red. Stalin waved his hand over the Soviet Union and exclaimed: 'Roosevelt and Churchill will never accept the idea that so great a space should be red, never, never!'

Source C: Churchill writing to Roosevelt shortly after the Yalta Conference

The Soviet Union has become a danger to the free world. A new front must be created against her onward sweep. This front should be as far east as possible. A settlement must be reached on all major issues between West and East in Europe before the armies of democracies melt away.

They disagreed:

• On how much Germany was to pay in reparations. Stalin wanted a much higher figure than either Roosevelt or Churchill. The decision was delayed until the next conference.

• About Poland – Stalin wanted the Polish/German border to be much further to the West than the western allies. He also wanted a 'friendly' Polish government so that his country would have some protection from Germany. The western powers feared that this would be a Soviet-controlled government. They persuaded Stalin to agree to allow free elections in Poland.

Tasks

1. *Does Source C support the evidence of Sources A and B about relations between the Big Three (the USA, the Soviet Union and Britain)? Explain your answer.*

2. *Describe one decision made about Germany at the Yalta Conference.*

The Potsdam Conference, July 1945

Changes between Yalta and Potsdam

In the five months between the conferences, a number of changes took place that greatly affected relations and the outcome of the conference at Potsdam.

- Soviet troops liberated countries in eastern Europe but did not remove their military presence. By July they occupied Latvia, Lithuania, Estonia, Finland, Czechoslovakia, Hungary, Bulgaria and Romania (see map on page 22).
- Stalin had set up a communist government in Poland, ignoring the wishes of the majority of Poles and the agreements made at Yalta. Stalin ignored protests from Britain and the USA. He insisted that his control of eastern Europe was a defensive measure against possible future attacks.

They agreed:

- To divide Germany and Berlin as previously agreed. Each of the four zones of Germany and four sectors of Berlin was occupied and administered by one of the Allies.
- To demilitarise Germany.
- To re-establish democracy in Germany including free elections, a free press and freedom of speech.
- That Germany had to pay reparations to the Allies in equipment and materials. Most of this would go to the Soviet Union, which had suffered most. The Soviet Union would be given a quarter of the industrial goods made in the western zones in return for food and coal from the Soviet zone.
- To ban the Nazi Party. Nazis were removed from important positions and leading Nazis were put on trial for war crimes at Nuremberg in 1946.
- To participate fully in the United Nations Organisation.
- That Poland's frontier was to be moved westwards to the rivers Oder and Neisse (see map on page 22).

- The Red Army was the biggest in the world, but Stalin refused to cut down his armed forces after the war. While there was **demilitarisation** in the West, the Soviet Union continued to expand its armed forces.

> **Source D:** Stalin speaking about the takeover of eastern Europe, 1945
>
> *This war is not as in the past. Whoever occupies a territory also imposes on his own beliefs and social system. Everyone imposes his own system as far as his army has power to do so. It cannot be otherwise.*

- In April 1945, Roosevelt died. His Vice-Pesident, Harry Truman, replaced him. Truman was totally different from Roosevelt and distrusted Stalin. He was convinced that the Soviet Union intended to take over the whole of Europe and was determined to stand up to the Soviet leader.
- On 16 July 1945, the Americans successfully tested an atomic bomb at a desert site in the USA. At the start of the Potsdam Conference, Truman informed Stalin about this. The Soviet leader was furious that he had not been consulted beforehand.
- Halfway through the Potsdam Conference, Churchill was defeated in the British general election and was replaced by Clement Attlee.

Attlee, Truman and Stalin (left to right) at the peace conference at Potsdam, July 1945

Tasks

3. What can you learn from Source D about Stalin's aims in eastern Europe?

4. Source E gives Attlee's views of Potsdam. What are his fears?

5. What do you think Truman would have said about Potsdam and Stalin? Put together a Source F – five or six lines from Truman about Potsdam. Remember that Truman was determined to prevent the spread of communism and ensure free elections.

6. Explain why relations between the USA and Soviet Union grew worse as a result of the peace conferences at Yalta and Potsdam.

They disagreed:
- Over what to do about Germany. Twenty million Russians had died during the war and Stalin wanted massive compensation that would have totally and permanently crippled Germany. Truman refused. He saw a revived Germany as a possible barrier to future Soviet expansion. Stalin wanted to disable Germany completely to protect the Soviet Union against future threats. Truman did not want Germany to be punished the way it had been by the **Treaty of Versailles** in 1919.
- About free elections. Truman wanted free elections in the countries of eastern Europe occupied by Soviet troops. Stalin refused to submit to US pressure believing it was unwelcome interference. Truman was furious and began a 'get tough' policy against the Soviet Union.

Who was to blame for the Cold War?

Soviet Union to blame

The Soviet Union was to blame because it was cold and harsh and was determined to spread the evil of communism as far as possible. It refused to allow free elections and set up Soviet-controlled communist governments in eastern Europe.

This view however, ignores Soviet concerns in 1945:

- Twice Russia had been invaded by Germany and suffered enormous losses of people. Germany had to be punished severely to ensure that it could not pose a future threat.
- The goal of Soviet expansion in eastern Europe was to create a buffer between Germany and the USSR. It was not to extend communism.
- Stalin was genuinely upset by Truman's announcement at Potsdam that the USA had the atomic bomb. As a result, the Americans would have the upper hand in any future arms race.

USA to blame

Soviet historians, on the other hand, blame the USA. The Americans failed to understand the suffering of the Soviet people during the Second World War and used the atomic bomb as a warning to the Soviet Union. The USA was concerned only about furthering its own interests in Eastern Europe.

This view, however, ignores US concerns:

- The Americans were genuinely concerned about Stalin's motives in eastern Europe, especially after he refused to allow free elections in Poland in 1945.
- The USA did not want to punish Germany severely. They remembered the lessons of 1919 and the harsh terms of the Treaty of Versailles.

Both to blame

It was due to a lack of mutual trust between the two Superpowers. Each side overreacted and made things worse by taking an aggressive stance, starting at Potsdam.

> **Source A:** Vyacheslav Molotov, Soviet Commissar of Foreign Relations, writing about the Potsdam Conference of July 1945
>
> *Truman decided to surprise us at Potsdam. He took Stalin and me aside and – looking secretive – informed us they had a secret weapon of a wholly new type, an extraordinary weapon. It's difficult to say what he was thinking, but it seemed to me that he wanted to throw us into consternation. Stalin, however, reacted to this quite calmly and Truman decided that he hadn't understood the words 'atomic bomb'.*

Source B: A British cartoon showing Stalin as the 'master of ceremonies' in front of 'the curtain'

Source C: A Soviet cartoon showing Europe being crushed by US capitalism

Source D: George Kennan was a US official in Moscow. In 1946 he wrote a long telegram to Truman warning the American president about the Soviet Union's determination to expand

It is clear that the United States cannot expect in the foreseeable future to be close to Soviet regime. It must continue to regard the Soviet Union as a rival, not a partner, in the political arena. It must continue to expect that Soviet policies will reflect no abstract love of peace and stability, no real faith in the possibility of a permanent happy coexistence of the communist and capitalist worlds. Rather, Soviet policies will be a cautious, persistent pressure toward the disruption and, weakening of all rival influence and rival power.

Tasks

1. *What can you learn from Source A about Stalin's reaction to being told about the atomic bomb?*

2. *Sources B and C are both examples of Cold War propaganda. What is the message of each cartoon?*

3. *Which sources*

- *suggest that the USA was to blame*
- *suggest that the Soviet Union was to blame?*

Give reasons for each choice.

4. *What do you think, based on the evidence so far? Using a scale of 1–5 (where 1 = little or no blame and 5 = strongly to blame), make a copy of the grid below and give your verdict with a brief explanation.*

	Rating 1–5	Explanation
Soviet Union		
USA		

5. *You are a either a Soviet or an American journalist. Use the appropriate headline below to write a brief article on the reasons for the Cold War (from the viewpoint of your country).*

US weapons threaten Soviet Union

Communism on the march in Eastern Europe

Examination practice

This section provides guidance on how to answer Question 1 on Paper 1.

Question 1 – two-mark question

Study Source A. Give **two** reasons from Source A why relations between the Allies 'continued to worsen' at the time of the Potsdam Conference. (Source A, line 1)

How to answer

This question is designed to test whether you can extract information from a source. The source may be from a textbook or it may be a picture or cartoon. The aim is **not** to display your knowledge so, in this case, it is a waste of your time to write all you know about Potsdam, the atom bomb or the names of the states that came under soviet control at that time.

Note that you are asked to find two reasons. You get one mark for each.

With only two marks available, write two short sentences and move on.

> **Source A:** From a school textbook published in 2001. It is describing the situation between the Allies at the Potsdam Conference in July, 1945.
>
> *Relations between the Allies continued to worsen. Stalin was told about the atom bomb, which increased his suspicions and fear of the West. At the same time, the Allies were worried about his take-over of eastern Europe. Soviet territory had expanded 480 kilometres westwards. They had taken over 22 million people who had not been in the USSR in 1939.*

Example
Stalin's fear of the west increased when he was told that they had developed an atomic bomb. The Allies were suspicious of soviet intentions because of the huge amount of territory which the USSR had taken over.

2 The early Cold War 1945–47

Source A: Part of a speech made by Winston Churchill at Fulton, Missouri, USA, March 1946

From Stettin in the Baltic to Trieste in the Adriatic, an iron curtain has descended across the continent of Europe. Behind that line lie all the capitals of the ancient states of central and eastern Europe. All these famous cities and the populations around them lie in the Soviet sphere and all are subject not only to Soviet influence but to a very high measure of control from Moscow.

Source B: A British cartoon of 1946 entitled 'A peep under the iron curtain'. The figure at the front represents Winston Churchill

Tasks

1. *What can you learn from Source A about Europe by 1946?*

2. *What message is the cartoonist trying to put across in Source B?*

In the years immediately following the end of the Second World War, the Soviet Union tightened its grip on those states in eastern Europe that it had liberated. This was seen by Britain and the USA as the beginning of Soviet expansion into western Europe. The USA retaliated with a policy of **containment** championed by President Truman together with a programme of economic aid to Europe known as the **Marshall Plan**.

This chapter answers the following questions:

- Why did the Soviet Union expand?
- How was Soviet control carried out, 1945–47?
- What were **Cominform** and **Comecon**?
- Why did US actions increase the rivalry?

Exam skills

This chapter gives guidance on how to answer Question 3 on Paper 1. This question, worth 10 marks, asks you to evaluate the usefulness of two sources.

Why did the Soviet Union expand?

A map showing Soviet expansion into eastern Europe

The Soviet Union expanded in 1945 for the following reasons:
- Memory of what happened 1918–39
- Percentages deal
- Strategic importance of Poland
- Security
- Expansionsim.

Memory of what happened 1918–39

During the interwar years most eastern European countries had been hostile to the Soviet Union. Poland had signed a non-aggression pact with France and during the Second World War Hungary and Romania fought on the side of Germany, against the Soviet Union.

Percentages deal

Towards the end of the war, Stalin and Churchill had reached an understanding known as the percentages deal (see Source A). Stalin believed that Churchill was accepting the influence of the Soviet Union in eastern Europe.

Strategic importance of Poland

The Soviet Union's future security was dependent on a friendly Polish government. Indeed, in 1945, Stalin wanted to move the Polish frontier so that most of Poland became part of the Soviet Union. He also wanted a communist government in what would remain of Poland. As Stalin said:
'For Russia it is not only a question of honour, but security – not only because we are on Poland's frontier, but also because throughout history, Poland has always been a corridor for attack on Russia.'

Security

The Soviet Union had been invaded from the west by Germany on two occasions, in 1914 and 1941, and had suffered huge casualties during the ensuing world wars. Stalin wanted to create a zone of 'friendly' or, better still, Soviet-controlled states in eastern Europe as a buffer against future invasions. As Stalin wrote in the Soviet newspaper *Pravda* in March 1946:

'The Soviet Union's loss of life has been several times greater than that of Britain and the United States put together. The Soviet Union cannot forget them. And so why is it surprising that the Soviet Union is anxious for its future safety and is trying to ensure that governments loyal to the Soviet Union should exist in these countries?'

Soviet expansionism

The USA, Britain and France believed that Stalin's motives were political – the expansion of the Soviet empire and communism throughout Europe.

Source B: A British cartoon showing Stalin overseeing communism throughout eastern Europe

Tasks

1. Describe one factor that influenced Soviet expansion into eastern Europe.

2. What message is the British cartoonist trying to put across in Source B?

3. Did the 'percentages deal' (Source A) give the Soviet Union dominant influence throughout eastern Europe? Explain your answer.

4. In what way would Britain and the USA have questioned Stalin's views about Poland?

How was Soviet control carried out, 1945–47?

Source A: A member of the Communist Party holding a gun threatens the Romanian opposition in Bucharest during the elections of 1946

Having freed much of eastern Europe from the Nazis, the Red Army remained in occupation and the Soviet Union established communist governments that were closely controlled from Moscow. These became known as Soviet **satellite states**. The same pattern was followed in each country:

- **Coalition governments** were set up in which the communists shared power with other political parties.
- Backed by Stalin, the communists took over the civil service, media, security and defence.
- Opposition leaders were arrested or forced to flee.
- Elections were held, but were fixed to ensure support for the communists.
- 'People's democracies' were set up.

Poland

In June 1945 a coalition government of several parties was set up. In January 1947 elections were rigged to ensure the election of a totally communist government. The leader of the main opposition party, Stanislaw Milokajcyk, fled to London.

Romania

As with Poland, a coalition government was set up in early 1945. Then in January 1945 the communists, encouraged by Stalin, took part in demonstrations to disrupt the government. Finally, in March 1945 the Soviet army intervened. It disarmed the Romanian army and forced the King to appoint a government dominated by the communists under Petru Groza. In November 1946 elections were held and the communists gained 80 per cent of the votes. In the following year the communist government abolished the monarchy.

Hungary

The largest party in 1945 was the Smallholders' Party, which won over 50 per cent of the vote in the elections of August 1945. However, the country began to experience an economic crisis, and the Communist Party was able to seize control of the Ministry of the Interior, which controlled the police. They used this control to great effect in 1947, arresting Bela Kovacs, the leader of the Smallholders' Party. The Prime Minister, Imre Nagy, was forced to resign. In the general election of August 1947, the communists secured a large share of the vote and took over the government. All other parties were then banned.

Czechoslovakia

The communists already had great support in Czechoslovakia. By 1947 they were the largest party in the coalition government and controlled the police and the armed forces. In 1948, supported by the Soviet Union, they used the army to seize control. Many non-communists were arrested and the foreign secretary, Jan Masaryk, a non-communist, was murdered. Rigged elections brought a communist victory. Soon after, all other political parties were banned.

Bulgaria

In late 1944 a communist-dominated government was set up. In November 1945 the communists won rigged elections and, in the following year, banned all other parties.

Yugoslavia

The communist resistance fought bravely against the Germans during the war. Its leader, Marshal Tito, was elected President. However, Tito had no intention of taking orders from Stalin. Yugoslavia was therefore expelled from the Communist International Bureau (Cominform) and other communist countries applied economic **sanctions**. To challenge Stalin further, Tito then accepted aid from the West.

What were the effects of Soviet expansion?

Britain and the USA were alarmed by Stalin's actions in eastern Europe. Roosevelt and Churchill had agreed that eastern Europe should be a 'Soviet sphere of influence' (see page 14) and that Stalin would heavily influence the region. However, they had not expected such complete Soviet domination. They were convinced that democratically elected governments, which would have also remained friendly to the Soviet Union, could have been set up in each country. This is when the major differences began to develop:

- Stalin believed that he could only ensure the support of the countries of eastern Europe by setting up Soviet-controlled communist governments.
- US President Truman saw this as a blatant attempt by Stalin to spread communism throughout Europe.

Source B: **A British cartoon of 1948 showing the Kremlin (government of the Soviet Union) in the background**

Tasks

1. *Describe one way in which Soviet expansion into eastern Europe affected relations with the West.*

2. *What can you learn from Source A about the elections in Romania in 1946?*

3. *What is the message of Source B? How does the cartoonist get the message across?*

4. *Draw your own cartoon or diagram giving a similar message about events in one of the other countries taken over by Soviet-controlled communists.*

What were Cominform and Comecon?

These two organisations were set up by the Soviet Union in the later 1940s in order to extend Soviet political and economic control over Eastern Europe.

Cominform	Comecon
The Communist Information Bureau was set up in 1947 to enable the Soviet Union to co-ordinate communist parties throughout Europe. It was the Soviet Union's response to the **Truman Doctrine** (see page 27). It was introduced to ensure that the states in Eastern Europe • followed Soviet aims in foreign policy • introduced Soviet style economic policies, such as **collectivisation of agriculture** and state control of industry. The Soviet Union used the organisation to **purge** any members who disagreed with Moscow. One notable example was Tito, whose refusal to follow the Soviet line led to the expulsion of Yugoslavia from Cominform in 1948 (see page 25).	The Council for Mutual Assistance (Comecon), founded in 1949, was the Soviet response to **Marshall Aid** (see pages 28–30). It was supposed to be a means by which the Soviet Union could financially support countries in Eastern Europe. In reality, it was used by the Soviet Union to: • control the economies of these states • give the Soviet Union access to their resources • encourage economic specialisation within the Soviet bloc. For example, Czechoslovakia and East Germany were encouraged to concentrate on heavy industry. Romania, Hungary and Bulgaria specialised in the production of food and raw materials.

Source A: A 1947 report by Andrei Zhdanov, the Leningrad Party boss, to the Cominform

The principal driving force of the imperialist camp is the USA. Allied with it are Great Britain and France. The cardinal purpose of the imperialist camp is to strengthen imperialism, to hatch a new imperialist war, to combat socialism and democracy, and to support reactionary and anti-democratic pro-fascist regimes and movements everywhere.

Source B: A view of Comecon from an issue of the US magazine *Time* published in 1960

COMECON. Founded eleven years ago in Moscow as a crude Stalinist device for milking the satellites for Soviet benefit. Soviet Russia, as the all-powerful supplier of the satellites' raw materials, calls all the COMECON tunes. All deals are bilateral, for there is no free exchange of goods in Communism's uncommon market.

Tasks

1. *Describe one feature of Cominform.*

2. *What, according to Source A, are the aims of the West?*
   Why would this report have been given to the first Cominform meeting?

3. *What does Source B suggest is the purpose of Comecon?*
   Is this is an accurate view of Comecon?

Why did US actions increase the rivalry?

The rivalry between the Superpowers intensified in 1947 due to the Truman Doctrine and the Marshall Plan.

The Truman Doctrine

In 1947 Truman began a US policy of containment. This was because:

- The USA, and especially Truman, believed that the Soviet Union was trying to spread communism – first through eastern Europe and then to the west and beyond.
- The USA had the atom bomb and wanted to use this, together with their superior economic strength, to put pressure on the Soviet Union and prevent further expansion.
- Events in Greece.

Greece

At Yalta, it was agreed that Britain would have influence in Greece. Since 1944 there had been a civil war in Greece, with Britain helping the **royalist government** to fight communist forces. In the Greek election of 1946, the communists were heavily defeated by royalists but the communists refused to give up. They continued to fight a **guerrilla war** against the Greek government and were helped by neighbouring communist countries.

Britain had 40,000 troops stationed in the country and gave money to the Greek government, as well as to Turkey, which was also under threat from communist rebels. By early 1947, Britain told the USA they could no longer afford to support the Greek and Turkish governments. The USA stepped in with the necessary financial aid fearing that these two countries would come under Soviet influence.

Truman announced US support in an important speech in March 1947. The speech marked a turning point in US foreign policy. In the interwar years and the two years since Potsdam, the USA had played little part in the affairs of Europe. Now Truman was committing the USA to a policy of containment that became known as the Truman Doctrine. In the first part of his speech, Truman argued that the world was becoming divided into two armed camps – the capitalist camp, which he claimed was the free camp, and the communist, which was not. The USA would use its economic and military strength to protect the world.

> **Source A: Part of a letter from Truman to James Byrne, Secretary of State, January 1946**
>
> *There isn't any doubt in my mind that Russia intends an invasion of Turkey. Unless Russia is faced with an iron fist and strong language, another war is in the making. I'm tired of babying the Soviets.*

> **Source B: The Truman Doctrine, 12 March 1947**
>
> *I believe that it must be the policy of the United States to support peoples who resist being enslaved by armed minorities or by outside pressure. I believe that we must help free peoples to work out their own destiny in their own way.*

Tasks

1. What does Source A reveal about Truman's attitude towards the Soviet Union?

2. What was meant by the 'Truman Doctrine'?

3. Briefly explain the key features of the Truman Doctrine.

4. Which country do you think Truman is referring to in the first sentence in Source B?

5. What is the message of Source C on page 28?

6. Describe one reason why the Truman Doctrine worsened relations between the two superpowers.

What were the consequences of the Truman Doctrine?

- The Greek government was able to defeat the communists.
- The rivalry between the USA and the Soviet Union increased. Truman had publicly stated that the world was divided between two ways of life: the free, non-communist and the unfree, communist. Within a year the first serious crisis of the Cold War would begin over Berlin.
- The USA became committed to the policy of containment and far more involved in European affairs.
- The USA decided on the Marshall Plan. Although an extremely generous act by the American people, it was motivated by US self-interest. The Americans wanted to create new markets for US goods.

- In 1947 Stalin set up the Communist Information Bureau, Cominform, to link communist parties in eastern Europe and worldwide, in common action.

The Marshall Plan

Truman backed up his policy of containment with economic aid to Europe. This was known as the 'Marshall Plan'.

Why was it introduced?

Truman did not want to commit the US military to the defence of western Europe against the spread of communism. He believed that communism generally won support in countries where there were economic problems, unemployment and poverty. Many European countries had suffered badly as a result of the Second World War and were struggling to deal with the damage caused. There were shortages of nearly everything, which led countries to implement rationing.

If the USA could help these countries to recover economically and provide employment and reasonable prosperity, then there would be no need to turn to communism. The plan, officially called the European Recovery Plan but nicknamed the Marshall Plan, was announced by the US Secretary of State, General George Marshall, in June 1947.

What aid was given?

The programme of aid was offered to all war-torn European countries to help them re-equip their

> Source C: A cartoon published in the British satirical magazine, *Punch*, in June 1947. The passengers, who represent the countries of Europe, are being given a choice of two buses. One is driven by Stalin and the other by Truman

> Source D: **Marshall announces the plan, June 1947**
>
> *Europe's requirements for the next three or four years of foreign foods and other essential products – mainly from the USA – are so much greater than its present ability to pay that it must have substantial additional help or face economic and political disaster. It is logical that the USA should do whatever it can to restore normal economic health to the world, without which there can be no political stability and peace. Our policy is directed not against any other country or political doctrine, but against hunger, poverty, desperation and chaos. Its purpose should be the revival of a working economy so as to produce the conditions in which free institutions can exist.*

factories and revive agriculture and trade. The USA offered money, equipment and goods to states willing to work together towards their economic recovery. This aid was in the form of cash, machinery, food and technological assistance. In return, they would agree to buy US goods and allow US companies to invest capital in their industries.

What were its results?

- Marshall invited countries to meet together and decide how to use US aid. Sixteen of these set up the Organisation for European Economic Recovery (OEEC) to put the Plan into action.
- By 1953 the USA had provided $17 billion to help them rebuild their economies and raise their standard of living. US machinery helped European factories to recover from the effects of the Second World War. US advisers helped to rebuild transport systems.
- Europe became more firmly divided between East and West. Stalin was initially involved but withdrew the Soviet Union from discussions because he did not trust the USA and did not want to show how weak the Soviet Union really was economically. He prevented eastern European countries, such as Czechoslovakia and Poland, from becoming involved.
- Stalin accused the USA of using the Plan for its own selfish interests – to dominate Europe and boost the US economy.

Source E: A graph showing the distribution of Marshall Aid

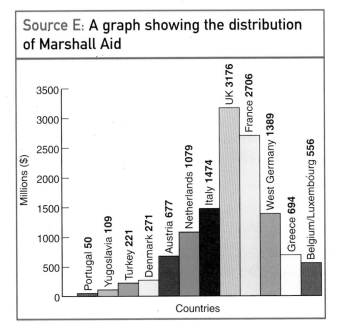

Source F: From Dean Acheson, a US adviser, speaking in 1945 about US aims in Europe

In the first place, our own interest is to maintain full employment and expand it sufficiently to absorb the twelve million or more men and women who will come back from the services. The great thing which creates purchasing power is people. If the people can develop their own countries in Europe, they will become an increasing market for US goods.

Source G: A speech by A. Vyshinsky, the deputy Soviet Foreign Secretary, September 1947, to the United Nations General Assembly

It is becoming more and more evident to everyone that the Marshall Plan will mean placing European countries under the economic and political control of the USA. It will mean direct interference by the USA in the internal affairs of those countries. The Plan is an attempt to split Europe into two camps and to complete the formation of a bloc of countries hostile to the Soviet Union.

Source H: A Soviet cartoon of 1949 commenting on the Marshall Plan

Source I: A view of the Marshall Plan by Soviet cartoonist Krokodil, 1947. European countries are on their knees before the USA, their paymaster

Source J: A cartoon drawn by E. H. Shepard and published in *Punch* on 1 October 1947

Source K: A photograph of Berliners using money from the Marshall Plan to help rebuild buildings destroyed during the war

Tasks

7. Describe one way in which the Marshall Plan helped the countries of western Europe.

8. Briefly explain the key features of the Marshall Plan.

9. Does Source F support the evidence provided by Sources D and G about the aims of the Marshall Plan?

10. Churchill claimed that the Marshall Plan was 'the most unselfish act in history'. Was the USA unselfishly trying to help Europe or were their motives less genuine?

- Make a copy of the grid below.
- Examine Sources D–K and complete the grid using evidence from the sources. An example has been done for you.
- Use your grid to write a 200-word answer to the question. Refer to the sources in your answer.

US motives for the Marshall Plan	
Selfish	

Examination practice

This section provides guidance on how to answer Question 3 on Paper 1. This is worth 10 marks and asks you to evaluate the usefulness of two sources as evidence for a particular enquiry.

There are **two** ways of judging the usefulness of a source, and for top marks you must do **both** for **both** sources. These are:

a) Its content. This is where you have to use your own knowledge to show that you understand the context from which the source comes. For example, does the source tell you a lot about the topic, or not? Is it typical? Is there important information which it does **not** mention?

b) Its Nature, Origin and Purpose. You will find the NOP in the **provenance** of the source. This is the important information included with the source which tells you what kind of source it is, when it was created, and why. You should use the NOP of the source to reach a judgement about its **value** and its **limitations**. An annotated example is given below.

Value

Content. The cartoon is useful because it includes a lot of details about the situation in 1947. Western European economies were indeed still in a poor state in 1947, finding it difficult to recover from all the damage caused by the Second World War. 'Self-help' is the little plank failing to prop up western Europe. The much bigger plank is being lifted at one end by General Marshall, but the USA was reluctant to support it. This is shown as 'Uncle Sam' – standing for the USA – sitting on the plank so it can't be moved.

Nature. This is a cartoon from a British magazine which cleverly includes a lot of detail about the situation in 1947. It is useful for giving the British view of the Marshall Plan. This was that the whole of western Europe was collapsing and needed American aid.

Origin. It is useful because it was published in 1947, when the USA was deciding whether to put the Marshall Plan into effect.

Source B: A cartoon drawn by E. H. Shepard and published in *Punch* on 1 October 1947

Purpose. It is useful because it shows how much Europeans wanted the Marshal Plan.

Limitations

Content. The cartoon represents the Marshall Plan as rescuing western Europe. But it also tied European economies to the USA. It was also very advantageous to the US economy which needed new markets for its own industry and a more prosperous Europe. .

Nature. This cartoon only represents the view of one person, E.H. Shepherd.

Origin. The cartoon was published in Punch. It may not be typical of the attitude of the British people, let alone everyone in western Europe.

Purpose. E.H. Shepherd is appealing to the American people to pass Marshall Aid. It doesn't say anything about opposition to the Plan.

Question 3 – ten-mark question

How useful are Sources B and C as evidence of the purpose of the Marshall Plan? Explain your answer, using Sources B and C and your own knowledge. (Source B is the cartoon on the previous page. Source C is below.)

Source C: A speech by A. Vyshinsky, the deputy Soviet Foreign Secretary, September 1947, to the United Nations General Assembly

It is becoming more and more evident to everyone that the Marshall Plan will mean placing European countries under the economic and political control of the USA. It will mean direct interference by the USA in the internal affairs of those countries. The Plan is an attempt to split Europe into two camps and to complete the formation of a bloc of countries hostile to the Soviet Union.

How to answer

Best answers deal systematically with both (a) the content and (b) the nature, origin and purpose (NOP) of both sources. Very best answers also have some of these features:

- A brief opening sentence that gives the 'big picture' of your answer.
- Items of own knowledge carefully selected and used to support judgements about what the sources say – their content – and their NOP.
- Statements about NOP to say whether they strengthen or weaken the evidence provided by the source.
- A brief conclusion.

Make a copy of the planning grid below and use it to plan your answer.

The writing frame below shows how to approach writing your answer.

Source B is useful because (contents) it suggests

....

Moreover Source B is also useful because of (NOP) ....

Source B has limitations/is unreliable because (contents) ....

Source B is also of limited use/is unreliable because (NOP) ....

Source C is useful because (contents) it suggests

....

Moreover Source C is also useful because of (NOP) ....

Source C has limitations/is unreliable because (contents) ....

Source C is also of limited use/is unreliable because (NOP) ....

In conclusion Sources B and C are useful because they ....

	Planning grid	
	Value	Limitations/Unreliability
Contents		
What does the source tell you?		
What view does the source tell you?		
NOP		
Nature		
Origin		
Purpose		

3 The Berlin crisis and its aftermath

Source A: A letter from a US citizen to President Truman in the early stages of the Berlin Crisis

Dear Sir,
The so-called 'Berlin Crisis' is entirely due to your own incredible stupidity when you allowed the Potsdam Conference to arrange final details for the occupation of Germany. It was your duty to look out for American interests and insist upon the establishment of a corridor to the American zone in the city. This you failed to do. Possibly this was because you believed Joe Stalin to be a 'good old chap', as you said some time ago. But I am inclined to think that you were too dumb to know that such a corridor was necessary. In the meantime, you seem willing and even eager to force this country into a war with Russia merely for the purpose of 'saving face'.

Source B: A photograph of an Allied plane delivering coal supplies in 1948, during the Berlin Blockade

Tasks

1. *What can you learn from Source A about the reasons for the Berlin Crisis?*

2. *Write a brief reply to the letter from Truman.*

3. *Why do you think Source B was widely publicised by the Allies?*

The build up of rivalry between East and West, in the years after 1945, culminated in the first major crisis of the Cold War, the Berlin Crisis of 1948–49. This confirmed the differences between the two sides, especially over the future of Germany. Furthermore, it encouraged the formation of two rival alliance systems, NATO for the West and the Warsaw Pact for the East.

This chapter answers the following questions:

• Why was there a crisis in Berlin in 1948–49 and what were its effects?
• How did developments in 1949–55 increase East-West rivalry?

Why was there a crisis in Berlin in 1948–49 and what were its effects?

In 1948 Stalin blockaded all routes by land and rail into West Berlin. This sparked the first major crisis of the Cold War and worsened relations between the Superpowers even further.

Long-term causes of the crisis

During the peace conferences (pages 14–17) of 1945, the Allies had agreed to divide both Germany and Berlin into four zones of occupation. Germany, however, was supposed to be kept as one country and to hold free elections. Almost immediately there were differences between the Soviet and western zones.

- The Soviet Union ensured that the minority communist group took control of their eastern zone. They tried, unsuccessfully, to secure communist control of the Berlin city council but the socialist majority, supported by the western powers, resisted successfully.
- The West wanted to speed up the economic recovery of Germany, which had been devastated by war and was now facing serious shortages of food and fuel. The Soviet Union wanted quite the opposite to secure itself from a future attack. It wanted to keep Germany weak and refused to allow its own zone to trade with the other three zones.
- Berlin was in the heart of Soviet-controlled East Germany. The western Allies were allowed access to their sectors by road, rail, canal and air. However, Stalin did not want the Allies inside Berlin, which was well within the Soviet zone. He also realised that the affluent, capitalist way of life would be on show to people in the East. Western countries were determined to remain in Berlin where they could observe Soviet activities on the other side of the Iron Curtain.

Short-term causes

The western Allies forged ahead by encouraging the economic recovery of their zones, especially in providing a much-needed currency. The western zones received large quantities of Marshall Aid (pages 28–29). In addition they set up free elections to establish democracy.

This was in sharp contrast with Soviet policies. Stalin feared a strong, democratic and reunited Germany on the borders of the Soviet Union. He feared that 'western' currency and democratic ideas would spread to the Soviet zone and undermine control of East Berlin.

A series of disagreements in the first half of 1948 brought about the crisis, as shown in the diagram below.

24 June Stalin accused the West of interfering in the Soviet zone. He cut off road, rail and canal traffic in an attempt to starve West Berlin. Stalin was trying to force the Allies to pull out of their sectors and abandon plans for separate development of their German zones.

June The western powers announced plans to create a West German State and introduced a new currency, the western Deutschmark, for their zones and West Berlin. The Soviet Union retaliated by introducing its own currency, the Ostmark, in the Soviet zone and East Berlin.

April The Allied zones were included in the Marshall Plan. Soviet troops began to hold up and search road and rail traffic entering West Berlin.

March Soviet representatives walked out of the **Allied Control Commission** complaining that Western attitudes made it unworkable. The Commission had been set up in 1945 to administer all the zones.

January The US and British zones in Berlin and Germany merged into one economic unit known as **Bizonia**.

The stages of the Berlin Crisis

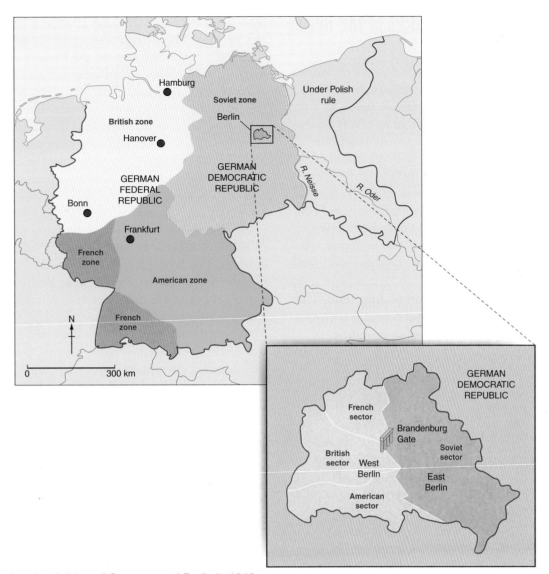

Map showing the division of Germany and Berlin in 1948

Task

1 *You are an adviser to the western powers and have been asked to weigh up the options facing them to deal with the blockade. Which option would you advise on?*

- *What are the advantages and disadvantages of each option? Use the following grid to help you:*

Options	Withdraw from Berlin	Supply Berlin by air
Advantages		
Disadvantages Drive through the blockade		

- *Write a memo to the western powers giving your recommended action.*
- *Give reasons for your choice.*

What were the key features of the Berlin airlift?

Truman was determined to stand up to the Soviet Union and show that he was serious about containment (see page 27). He saw Berlin as a test case. If the western Allies gave in to Stalin on this issue, the western zones of Germany might be next. Truman wanted Berlin to be a symbol of freedom behind the Iron Curtain.

The only way into Berlin was by air. So the Allies decided to airlift supplies from their bases in West Germany. Would the Soviet Union shoot down these planes? There were anxious moments as the first planes flew over Berlin but no shots were fired.

Source A: A British cartoon of July 1948. The man holding the gun is Stalin and the storks represent the planes carrying supplies

THE BIRD WATCHER

The airlift began on 28 June 1948 and lasted for ten months. The British codenamed it 'Operation Plainfare'. It was the start of the biggest airlift in history. Soon planes were flying day and night along the air corridors. Each was given an exact time to land at 90-second intervals. The pilots had a dangerous job as Soviet planes flew across the air corridors and weather balloons were placed in awkward positions. As a warning to the Soviet Union, Truman ordered B-29 bombers, capable of carrying atom bombs, to be sent to Britain. The Soviet Union was now within US bombing range.

By September the planes were flying 4600 tons of supplies a day – although this was still not enough. The Soviet Union even tried to persuade people to move from West to East Berlin. Only three per cent took up the offer. Stalin hoped that severe winter conditions would paralyse the airlift. However it was a relatively mild winter that did not disrupt the flights.

The airlift continued into the spring and reached its peak on 16–17 April 1949 when 1398 flights landed nearly 13,000 tons of supplies in 24 hours.

Source B: Report by Arthur Henderson, the British Secretary for Air, May 1949

In the 318 days since the Airlift began, British and American aircraft have made 195,350 flights to Berlin, carrying 1,583,686 tonnes of supplies. British aircraft have made 63,612 flights carrying 369,347 tonnes – made up of 185,000 tonnes of food, 97,000 tonnes coal, 50,000 tonnes of fuel, 21,000 tonnes of miscellaneous goods and 15,000 tonnes of supplies for the British services in Berlin.

During the airlift West Berliners were supplied with everything from food and clothing to oil and building materials, although there were still great shortages in the city and many decided to leave. During this period there was a total of 275,000 flights with an average of 4000 tonnes of supplies each day.

On 12 May 1949 Stalin called off the blockade. He had failed to starve the Allies out of Berlin. That evening Berliners put on evening dress and danced in the streets.

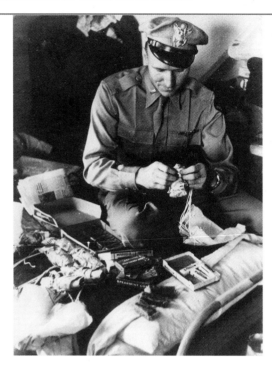

What were the results of the crisis?

The crisis had three major effects:

- It greatly increased East-West rivalry.
- It confirmed the divisions of Germany and Berlin.
- It led to the creation of the North Atlantic Treaty Organisation or NATO (see page 39).

East–West rivalry

Truman saw the crisis as a great victory (see Source D). West Berlin had survived and stood up to the Soviet Union. For Stalin it was a defeat and a humiliation, although this was not what the Soviet people were led to believe (see Source E).

Source D: Truman speaking in 1949

We refused to be forced out of the city of Berlin. We demonstrated to the people of Europe that we would act and act resolutely, when their freedom was threatened. Politically it brought the people of western Europe closer to us. The Berlin blockade was a move to test our ability and our will to resist.

Source E: The Soviet version of the crisis written in 1977

The crisis was planned in Washington behind a smokescreen of anti-Soviet propaganda. In 1948 there was danger of war. The conduct of the western powers risked bloody incidents. The self-blockade of the western powers hit the West Berlin population with harshness. The people were freezing and starving. In the Spring of 1949 the USA was forced to yield. Their war plans had come to nothing, because of the conduct of the Soviet Union.

Germany

Germany was now clearly divided. Within a few days of the end of the Berlin crisis, in May 1949, the western Allies announced that their former occupation zones, including west Berlin, would join together to form the Federal Republic of Germany (FRG) (see map on page 35). Stalin's response was rapid and in October 1949 the Soviet zone became the German Democratic Republic (GDR).

Tasks

2. What can you learn from Source B about the Berlin airlift?

3. a) What message is the cartoonist in Source A trying to get across?

   b) Why do you think Stalin decided not to shoot down the storks?

4. Source C is a photograph which was shown in Allied newspapers. Devise a propaganda caption to go with the photograph.

5. Does Source E support the evidence of Source D about the Berlin Crisis? Explain your answer.

6. What changes would you make to Source E to make it a more accurate version of the events of the crisis?

7. Put together contrasting newspaper headlines announcing the end of the airlift (one from a Soviet and one from a US perspective).

How did developments in 1949–55 increase East-West rivalry?

The Cold War and East-West rivalry increased even more in the years after the Berlin Crisis with the formation of rival alliance systems and the arms race.

By the mid 1950s the USA and Soviet Union were members of two rival alliance systems, NATO and the Warsaw Pact.

North Atlantic Treaty Organisation (NATO)

The Berlin Crisis had confirmed Truman's commitment to containment in Europe and highlighted the Soviet threat to western Europe. western European states, even joined together, were no match for the Soviet Union and needed the formal support of the USA. In April 1949 the North Atlantic Treaty Organisation was signed. Although a defensive alliance, NATO's main purpose was to prevent Soviet expansion.

A map of American and Soviet 'spheres of influence' across Europe

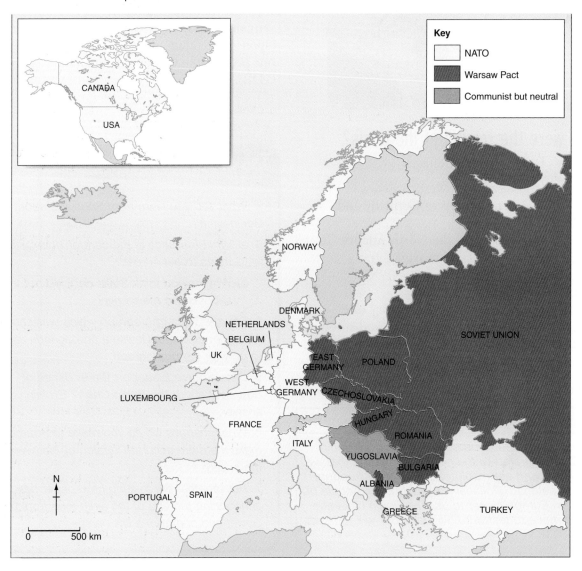

Source A: A Soviet cartoon showing the NATO generals goose-stepping. This had been the Nazi method of marching. The overall commander in the foreground is carrying a nuclear bomb and a portrait of Hitler

Рис. КУКРЫНИКСЫ

ИЗ СЕРИИ

Палачи.

Справа налево: Эйзенхауэр, Брэдли, Риджуэй, Монтгомери, де Латтр де Тассиньи, Жуэн, Гудериан, Гальдер, Фрэзер, Коллинс, Тито.

Task

1. *Here are some of the consequences of the setting up of NATO.*

- *The USA was now committed to the defence of Western Europe.*
- *Stalin did not believe it was a defensive alliance. He believed it was aimed against the Soviet Union.*
- *It intensified the arms race between the two sides and the development of ever more powerful weapons of destruction (see page 40).*
- *Within six years the Soviet Union set up the Warsaw Pact.*
- *Eventually the USA set up its own missile bases in Western Europe, including the UK.*

Draw a mind map prioritising these consequences from most to least important by completing the following steps:

  a) *Central box 'consequences of NATO'*
  b) *Place the consequences clockwise starting at 12.00 from the most important to least important*
  c) *Briefly explain your choices.*

Source B: Extracts from the NATO charter

Article 3: To achieve the aims of the Treaty, the Parties will keep up their individual and collective capacity to resist armed attack.
Article 5: The Parties agree that an armed attack against one or more of them in Europe or North America shall be considered an attack against them all.

Tasks

2. *What message is the cartoonist trying to get across in Source A?*

3. *What can you learn from Source B about the aims of NATO?*

The Warsaw Pact

Stalin saw NATO as an 'aggressive alliance' aimed against the Soviet Union. Within six years, in 1955, the Soviet Union had set up its own rival organisation known as the Warsaw Pact. It was a military alliance of eight nations headed by the Soviet Union and was designed to counter the threat of NATO. Members were to support each other if attacked. A joint command structure was set up under the Soviet Supreme Commander.

Why did the Hungarian uprising take place?

Task

1. Look at Source A. What do you think that Khrushchev meant when he stated: 'the Soviet Union cannot ... allow a breach in the front of eastern Europe'?

Hungary after the Second World War

The Soviet Union invaded Hungary, one of Hitler's allies, in September 1944 as it drove Nazi forces back towards Germany. Soviet troops occupied Hungary and continued to do so after the end of the war even though an Allied Control Commission for Hungary was set up to run the country. The Control Commission comprised the Soviet Union, the USA and the UK. However, the Soviet Union was the most influential of the powers and was able to determine events in Hungary in the immediate post-war years.

A new Provisional Government was set up near the end of the war and it agreed to pay the Soviet Union reparations of $300 million. Elections were held in November 1945, in which the independent Smallholders' Party won 57 per cent of the vote, while the Hungarian Communist Party secured only 17 per cent. The head of the occupying Soviet forces, Marshal Voroshilov, refused to allow the Smallholders' Party to establish a government and he established a coalition that contained members of the Hungarian Communist Party.

Laszlo Rajk, a member of the Communist Party, was in charge of the security police.

The impact of Soviet control

In February 1947, some leaders of the Smallholders' Party and National Peasant Party were arrested and others fled Hungary as a result of Soviet pressure and control. In the ensuing elections, the Communist Party became the largest single party but, because it did not have a majority, it served in the coalition government.

A new constitution based on the Soviet Union system was drawn up, making Hungary a '**republic of workers and working peasants**'. Matyas Rakosi emerged from the Communist Party to lead Hungary, and he began to impose a dictatorial rule, calling himself a follower of Stalin. Hungary became a member of Cominform (see page 26) and the Hungarian Communist Party took its orders from Moscow.

The rule of Rakosi

Rakosi used terror and brutality to keep control, killing an estimated 2000 in the purges and imprisoning 200,000 political opponents. The secret police (AVH) became a hated and dreaded part of Hungarian life. To further Rakosi's control, religious teaching in schools was attacked and removed from the education system. Cardinal Mindszenty, the leader of the Hungarian Catholic Church, was imprisoned for life in 1949.

The Hungarian economy was controlled by the Soviet Union through Comecon. This body prevented Hungary trading with western Europe and receiving any Marshall Aid (see pages 28–30). Therefore, like the other satellite states of eastern Europe, Hungary was forced to trade on uneven terms with the Soviet Union. This meant that Hungary did not always receive a fair price for its exports there.

Rakosi put forward a Five-Year Plan to transform the economy of Hungary, but it failed to bring real progress. The plan was devoted to heavy industry and the production of steel, but Hungary had no iron ore or coking coal with which to produce steel. Living standards began to fall, and in 1952 Hungary experienced its lowest agricultural output ever. Rakosi became increasingly unpopular.

When Stalin died, the new leader of the Soviet Union, Malenkov, did not favour Rakosi, who was replaced by Imre Nagy. This shows the control that the Soviet Union had in Hungary. During the next three years there was much change in Hungary. The time chart below indicates key events.

Tasks

2. *Create a spider diagram to show the ways in which Rakosi kept control of Hungary's people.*

3. *Why were Comecon and Cominform important for the Soviet Union in their control over Hungary?*

4. *Look at the table below. Explain which events:*

   a) *encouraged the Hungarians to challenge the Soviet Union.*
   b) *concerned the Soviet Union about their control of eastern Europe.*

DATE	EVENT
1953	
March	Death of Stalin
	Rakosi replaced by Imre Nagy as Prime Minister
1955	
April	Nagy replaced by Rakosi
May	Warsaw pact set up (see page 40)
1956	
February	Khrushchev's 'secret speech'
July	Rakosi forced from power on the orders of Moscow and succeeded by his close friend Erno Gero
October	Victims of Rakosi's purges were re-buried
23 October	Students demonstrated in Budapest, the capital of Hungary, demanding free elections, free press and the withdrawal of Soviet troops. Statue of Stalin was pulled down in Budapest and dragged through the streets.

A table showing the key dates in the Hungarian uprising

Stalin's statue is toppled in Budapest in 1956

What were the key features of the uprising?

After the demonstrations began in October 1956, Khrushchev sent troops and tanks to Budapest to try to restore peace, and on 25 October the tanks opened fire killing twelve and wounding more than a hundred people. On that day, Gero was forced to resign and Janos Kadar took over as temporary prime minister. The following day Nagy was re-instated as prime minister.

Nagy held talks with the Soviet Union and it was agreed that the tanks would be withdrawn. John Foster Dulles, the US Secretary of State, said: 'You can count on us'. The Hungarians interpreted this as a sign that the USA would support them against the Soviet Union if help were ever needed. However, President Eisenhower (who succeeded Truman in 1953) was careful about committing the USA because he had no wish to become involved in any dispute during the forthcoming presidential election.

Nagy released some political prisoners on 30 October, the most famous of these being Cardinal Mindszenty. The following day Nagy's proposed reforms were published. His most controversial decision was his intention to withdraw Hungary from the Warsaw Pact.

Moreover, Nagy asked the United Nations (UN) to consider Hungary's disputes with the Soviet Union. He hoped to win support at the UN and felt that the Soviet Union would be drawn into negotiations. Political parties that had been banned under Rakosi now re-appeared, and Nagy announced a coalition government on 3 November.

- Free elections
- Hungary to develop trade links with the West
- An end to the one-party system
- Freedom of the press
- Freedom of speech
- Freedom of worship
- Hungary to become a neutral state
- Free trade unions

What the Hungarians were fighting for

Khrushchev was anxious not to be seen as weak by other members of the Warsaw Pact. Furthermore, Mao Zedong, the Chinese leader, was urging him to stand firm against any deviation from communism. Khrushchev decided that Nagy had gone too far, and on 4 November 200,000 Soviet troops and 6000 tanks returned to Hungary. The Soviet army quickly captured airports, bridges and key road junctions but, in spite of this, the Hungarians fought on using guerrilla tactics. There was bitter fighting but the rebels were no match for the Soviet forces. A ceasefire was agreed for 10 November but there was sporadic fighting until the middle of 1957.

Source A: From a radio message sent by Hungarian rebels during the fighting, early November 1956

We have almost no weapons, no heavy guns of any kind. The Hungarian people are not afraid of death. You can't let people attack tanks with their bare hands. What is the United Nations doing?

Source B: A radio broadcast made by the rebels in early November 1956

Civilised people of the world! Our ship is sinking. Light is fading. The shadows grow darker over the soil of Hungary. Help us!

As the crisis raged in Hungary, world attention was drawn away to events in the Middle East, where British and French forces had landed at the Suez Canal and Israeli troops had invaded Egypt through the Sinai desert. The USA was keen to have Britain and France remove their troops and the invasion was a fortunate diversion for Khrushchev.

Janos Kadar became Hungary's new leader. Nagy had been hiding in the Yugoslav embassy during the fighting. Kadar offered him safe passage out of the country. However, Kadar broke his word and arrested Nagy, who was then taken to Romania and shot in 1958.

Source C: Photograph of Hungarian rebels, 4 November 1956

Source D: From *Time* magazine, a US political publication, 14 November 1956. It is describing Soviet actions in Hungary

The steel covered Soviet boot trod on Hungary this week, stamping and grinding out the young democracy.

Tasks

1. Look at Sources A, B and C. What can you learn about the rebels from these sources?

2. Look at Source D. What is the attitude of the USA to the Soviet Union's action in Hungary?

3. Look at the diagram to the left showing the reasons behind the Soviet invasion of Hungary. Put the reasons in order of importance and explain your decision carefully.

Pressure from Mao and China to protect Communism from the West

Presidential elections

Khrushchev needed to stamp his authority on the Soviet Union

WHY DID THE SOVIET UNION INVADE HUNGARY?

Set example to rest of eastern Europe

Damage to the Warsaw Pact

USA and UN involved in the Suez Crisis

Fear of loss of control of eastern Europe

What were the results of the uprising?

Soviet troops were easily able to defeat the rebels, but at a cost. About 7000 of them were killed, though the rebels lost at least 20,000. Khrushchev was able to keep control, and a new Soviet-backed leader, Kadar, was installed. About 200,000 Hungarians fled the country during the uprising. Many came to Britain as political refugees.

The Soviet Union had maintained its empire and sent out a warning to any satellite state thinking of breaking away. Khrushchev's policy of **de-Stalinisation** would only go as far as he wanted it to. Poland and Hungary made only slow and gradual reforms after 1956 but remained firmly under the yoke of the Soviet Union. The West saw Khrushchev's recent messages of peace as a sham.

Source A: A photograph showing Hungarian refugees fleeing to Austria in November 1956, after the Hungarian uprising

Source B: The front page of the *Daily Mail*, an English newspaper, from 5 November 1956

Source C: From *Pravda*, the Soviet state newspaper, 23rd November 1956

A communist state could not remain a silent observer to the bloody reign of Fascist reaction in People's Democratic Hungary. When everything settles down in Hungary and life becomes normal again, the Hungarian working class, peasantry and intelligentsia will undoubtedly understand our actions better and judge them right. We see our help to the Hungarian working class in its struggle against counter-revolution as our international duty.

Tasks

1. *Imagine that the Soviet Union had published Source A. Devise a caption a Soviet writer might have used.*

2. *What does Source B tell us about British attitudes to the Hungarian uprising?*

3. *Would the majority of Hungarian people agree with the views expressed in Source C? Explain your answer.*

4. *Re-read the text on the results of the uprising. Consider what the effects of it were and then copy this table and fill in the boxes.*

Effects for Hungary	Effects for the Soviet Union	Effects for Superpower relations

Examination practice

This section gives guidance on how to answer Question 2 on Paper 1.

Question 2 – four-mark question

Outline two ways in which the Soviet Union controlled Hungary before 1956.

How to answer

- Notice that the question starts with the word 'outline': the examiners are not looking for an essay here, but for a simple, clear statement.
- Then notice that this is a four-mark question. That means two marks for each of your two statements – one for the main point, and another for good additional detail. A full marks response might be:

> The Soviet Union forced Hungary to belong to Comecon, the economic union of all states under soviet control. They had to develop industries which did not suit Hungary, a food-producing country, and sell their produce at low, fixed prices.
>
> The question of who ruled Hungary was decided in Moscow, not Budapest. Rakosi, who made himself dictator of Hungary in 1947 was a loyal follower of Stalin. When Stalin died in 1953, Rakosi was replaced by Imre Nagy two years later.

Now have a go yourself:

Outline two steps which Khrushchev took to re-establish soviet control of Hungary.

2 Three Cold War crises: Berlin, Cuba and Czechoslovakia 1957–69

Source A: An extract from a speech made in 1953 by John Foster Dulles, the US Secretary of State. He was talking about the Soviet threat

We shall never have a secure peace or happy world so long as Soviet communism dominates one third of all the people of the world and continues to try to extend its rule to many others. Therefore, we must always have in mind the liberation of these captive people.

Task

What can you learn from Source A about the relationship between the USA and the Soviet Union?

By 1956, the development of two opposing armed groups was clear for the world to see. Put simply, it was seen as West versus East, **communism** against capitalism and, most importantly, the USA versus the Soviet Union. The three studies in this chapter define the Cold War – showing the brutality, callousness and **brinkmanship** of this period in history. The climax of the Cold War came with the Cuban Missiles Crisis in 1962, when the world stood at the very edge of nuclear war.

Each chapter within this section explains a key issue and examines important lines of enquiry as outlined below.

Chapter 5 Berlin: a divided city (pages 49–54)

- What were the causes of the Berlin Crisis of 1961?
- What were the key features of the crisis?
- What were the results of the crisis?

Chapter 6 Cuba: the world on the brink of war (pages 55–64)

- What were the causes of the Cuban Missiles Crisis of 1962?

- What were the key features of the crisis?
- What were the results of the crisis?

Chapter 7 Czechoslovakia: the Prague Spring (pages 65–73)

- Why was there opposition to Soviet control of Czechoslovakia?
- What were the key features of the Soviet invasion?
- What were the consequences of the Soviet invasion?

5 Berlin: a divided city

Source A: US tanks (foreground) facing Soviet tanks (top of photograph) at Checkpoint Charlie, Berlin 1961

Source B: Residents of West Berlin look over the newly built Wall into East Berlin, August 1961

Tasks

1. *What can you learn about the Berlin crisis of 1961 from Source A?*

2. *What can you learn about Berlin in 1961 from Source B?*

3. *Devise Soviet and US propaganda captions for Sources A and B.*

Chapter 3 explored how Berlin created problems for the wartime Allies. The Blockade and Airlift were indications of the huge gulf that had grown between the allies by 1949. After the creation in 1949 of West Germany (the Federal Republic) and East Germany (the Democratic Republic), Berlin remained a divided and occupied city. The Soviet Union's desire to remove the Western Allies from Berlin created a crisis in 1961. This crisis led to the construction of the Berlin Wall.

This chapter answers the following questions:

• Why did the Soviet Union wish to control Berlin?
• What were the results of the crisis?

What were the causes of the Berlin Crisis of 1961?

Problems in East Germany

You have already read in Chapters 2 and 3 about the division of Berlin in 1945 and the Berlin airlift in 1948–49. Even after 1949, Berlin continued to pose a problem for the USA and Soviet Union. This was especially true for the Soviet Union, who wanted to remove the Allies from West Berlin because it was an area of capitalist prosperity and a symbol of the success of western Europe within communist territory. Between 1949 and 1961, about 4 million East Germans fled to the West through Berlin. Berlin was a gap in the Iron Curtain, and the Soviet Union was keen to block this gap up. Furthermore, the Soviet Union claimed that the USA and its Allies used West Berlin as a base for espionage. The Soviets argued that they needed to control movement and access into Berlin in order to combat Western espionage.

East Germans fled to the West because they were dissatisfied with economic and political conditions at home. The forced **collectivisation of agriculture** and the end of private trading were not popular among the people of East Germany. Moreover, there were shortages of consumer goods, which could be bought cheaply in West Berlin.

The views of Eisenhower and Khrushchev

In 1958 Khrushchev issued the **Berlin Ultimatum**. He accused the Allies of breaking the Potsdam Agreement, telling them that they should leave Berlin within 6 months, and suggesting that it should become a neutral free city. President Eisenhower of the USA seemed prepared to negotiate. He did not want to risk a war over Berlin. Khrushchev's visit to the USA in 1959 seemed to be successful, and a summit conference at Camp David was agreed to discuss Berlin and **nuclear weapons**.

Khrushchev and Eisenhower were set to meet in Paris on 14 May 1960. Nine days before the summit conference was due to open, the Soviet Union announced that it had shot down an American U-2 spy plane near the city of Sverdlovsk. The pilot was captured and put on trial. Khrushchev demanded that all such flights stop and that the USA give an apology for spying. Eisenhower was prepared to stop the flights but would not apologise. There were bitter exchanges between Khrushchev and Eisenhower at a preliminary meeting, which ended with Khrushchev storming out of the first session. Eisenhower immediately cancelled his planned visit to the Soviet Union. Relations were growing very cold.

How did Khrushchev challenge the USA?

Several issues concerning West Germany created anxieties for Khrushchev. In 1955 West Germany had joined NATO (see pages 38–39), and in 1957 it had joined the European Economic Community. Not only was West Germany economically strong and growing stronger, it was seen by Khrushchev as a military threat. The Soviet Union's fear of another German invasion would not go away.

Hence Khrushchev was determined to solve the problem of Berlin. For him, Berlin was 'a fishbone stuck in his throat'. From January 1961, the number of refugees leaving East Berlin for the West increased rapidly to more than 20,000 a month. Large numbers of these refugees were professional people (on one day, for example, the entire Mathematics Department of the University of Leipzig defected), but there were also many skilled craftsmen among them. This drain of labour and economic output threatened to bring about the economic collapse of East Germany.

Continuing to seek a solution, Khrushchev fixed another summit conference with the new president of the USA – John F. Kennedy. Khrushchev felt that he would be able to use his experience to push the young Kennedy around. However, he had failed to note that Kennedy had re-asserted the **Truman Doctrine** (see pages 27–28) in his **inauguration speech** on 20 January 1961.

At the Vienna summit of June 1961, Khrushchev again demanded that western forces leave West Berlin. He said he would make a treaty with East Germany which would end all occupation rights, including Western access to Berlin. Kennedy refused to withdraw western forces and increased US defence spending by $3.5 billion the following month.

In July, Khrushchev announced that the Soviet defence budget would be increased by more than 30 per cent. On 13 August 1961, Khrushchev closed the border between East and West Berlin, and East German police placed barbed wire along the 50-kilometre line dividing the two sections. As the day progressed, construction of a concrete wall got under way, and it was completed by the next day. Eventually, the whole of West Berlin was encircled. The term 'Iron Curtain' was a metaphor, but the Berlin Wall was real. The USA and its Allies did nothing to stop the building of the Wall.

Source A: From a speech by President Eisenhower in September 1959

*There must be some way to develop some kind of free city that might be part of West Germany. Perhaps the **United Nations** would guarantee the freedom, safety and security of the city... The time is coming, and perhaps soon, when we would simply have to get our forces out.*

Source B: Khrushchev speaking at the Paris press conference in May 1960. Khrushchev, who was hissed and booed, thought the noises came from the German press

You fascist bastards are the kind we did not finish off at Stalingrad. We hit you so hard that we put you ten feet under right away. If you boo us and attack us again, look out! We will hit you so hard there won't be a squeal out of you.

Source C: From a radio speech by Kennedy to the US people on 25 July 1961

We cannot and will not permit the communists to drive us out of Berlin, either gradually or by force. There is peace in Berlin today. The source of trouble and tension is Moscow, not Berlin. We seek peace but we shall not surrender.

Source D: Khrushchev at the press conference which revealed the Paris Summit would not go ahead. Khrushchev was aggressive to the German reporters. On Khrushchev's left is the Defence Minister, Marshal Malinovsky

Source E: From a conversation between Khrushchev and a US diplomat at the end of July 1961

If your troops try to force their way to Berlin, we will oppose them by force. War is bound to go thermonuclear, and though you and I may survive, all your European allies will be completely destroyed.

Tasks

1. Re-read these pages and pages 34–37. Write a newspaper article from the Soviet point of view, explaining why Western Allies should leave Berlin.

2. What can you learn from Source A about Eisenhower's attitude to the problem of Berlin?

3. Describe one reason why the Soviet Union wanted the Allies to leave West Berlin.

4. What can you learn about Khrushchev as a leader from Sources B and D?

5. Look at Sources C and E. What can you learn about the Cold War from these sources?

6. *Explain why Khrushchev thought his case for ejecting the West from Berlin was growing stronger.*

7. *Describe one way in which relations between the USA and Soviet Union worsened in the period before the Berlin Wall was built.*

8. *What is meant by the term 'Iron Curtain'?*

9. *Look at Sources E (page 51), F and G. Can you suggest reasons why the USA did not oppose the building of the Wall?*

Source F: Map showing the Berlin Wall encircling West Berlin

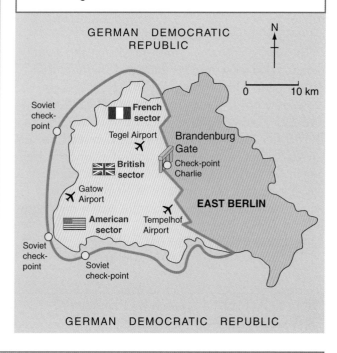

Source G: Photograph of East German workers building the Wall, August 1961. They are placing pieces of glass on top of the blocks

What were the results of the crisis?

Peace was maintained, but at a price for the German people. Families were split, and travel restrictions made it very difficult for relatives to see one another. Germans also felt let down because the Soviet Union had broken the 1949 agreement about the running of Berlin, and for all his bluster, Kennedy had not gone to war.

> **Source A:** From a conversation between Kennedy and an aide after the Vienna Summit in 1961
>
> *It seems particularly stupid to risk killing a million Americans over an argument about access rights on an Autobahn [German motorway] or because Germans want Germany re-unified. If I'm going to threaten the Soviet Union with nuclear war, it will have to be for bigger and more important reasons than that.*

Khrushchev interpreted the construction of the Wall in two ways. He felt that he had beaten Kennedy and was prepared for the next chance to out-manoeuvre his rival. The flow of refugees was stopped, and the economic crisis East Germany was facing slowly evaporated. Khrushchev said that the Wall was 'guarding the gates of socialist paradise'.

Although Khrushchev had failed to remove western forces from Berlin, the crisis ended and tension in Europe was eased.

The Wall became the symbol of the division in the world and, for Berliners, it was a constant reminder that their country was still a tool of the Superpowers. President Kennedy visited West Germany in 1963. He made several speeches in some of its major cities, where he was met by huge, cheering crowds. When he moved on to West Berlin, he embarked on a thirty-mile tour of the main streets, which were lined with an estimated 1.5 million people (out of a population of about 2.5 million). He spoke to a crowd of about 200,000 in the centre of the city, near the Wall. Some East Berliners listening to him on the other side of the Wall applauded him, too.

> **Source B:** From President Kennedy's speech in West Berlin, 28 June 1963
>
> *While the wall is the most obvious and vivid demonstration of the failures of the Communist system, for all the world to see, we take no satisfaction in it. For it is, as your Mayor has said, an offence not only against history but an offence against humanity, separating families, dividing husbands and wives and brothers and sisters, and dividing a people who wish to be joined together… Freedom has many difficulties and democracy is not perfect, but we have never had to put a wall up to keep our people in, to prevent them from leaving us. There are many people in the world who really don't understand, or say they don't, what is the great issue between the free world and the communist world. Let them come to Berlin. Today, in the world of freedom, the proudest boast is 'Ich bin ein Berliner'.*
>
> (Although Kennedy meant this to mean: 'I am a Berliner', he should have said in German: 'Ich bin Berliner'. Outside Berlin, a Berliner – ein Berliner – is a German pastry; some people joke that he actually said: 'I am a jelly doughnut'.)

> **Source C:** Citizens of West Berlin lifting their children so that relatives in the East may see them. The photograph was taken in late 1961

Source D: Cartoon about Khrushchev and the Berlin Wall. A possible caption might read: 'See how many are staying on our side'

Source E: An unarmed Berlin teenager was shot and killed by East German guards as he tried to escape to West Berlin over the wall, August 1962

Tasks

1. *Kennedy was accused of being tough on Cuba but soft on Berlin. Explain what was meant by this. (Read Chapter 6 to help you answer this question.)*

2. *Imagine you are a West Berliner. Write a letter to President Kennedy explaining why you think that the USA should intervene to reunite Berlin.*

3. *Create your own caption for Source D.*

4. *Using Sources A–E and the text on pages 53–54, copy and complete the table below about the effects of the Berlin Wall. An example has been done for you.*

Effects for Germany	Effects for the Soviet Union	Effects for Superpower relations
	Source D was bad publicity for the Soviet Union – showed their inhumanity to the world.	

6 Cuba: the world on the brink of war

Tasks

1. *What can you learn from Source A about the impact of the Cuban Missiles Crisis?*

2. *Interview grandparents and other people who lived through the Cuban Missiles Crisis. What do they remember of the crisis?*

Chapter 5 explored the deterioration in relations between the USA and the Soviet Union as a result of the Berlin Crisis. President Kennedy had stated his belief that Berlin was not worth going to war over (see Source A on page 53). However, the Cold War continued to grow colder with the development of the arms race and the hawkish attitude of Khrushchev. The climax of the Cold War came in October 1962, when the Soviet Union placed nuclear missiles on the island of Cuba. The Superpowers were on the brink of nuclear war, and for almost two weeks the world held its breath. Fortunately, the USA and Soviet Union were able to find a solution to the crisis. The following years saw closer relations between them and eventually a period of *détente*.

This chapter answers the following questions:

- In what ways did the arms race develop in the 1950s?
- What were the causes of the Cuban Missiles Crisis?
- What were the key features of the crisis?
- What were the results of the crisis?

Exam skills

This chapter gives guidance on how to answer Question 4 on Paper 1. This question is worth six marks and asks you to provide a description from your own knowledge.

In what ways did the arms race develop in the 1950s?

The preceding chapters have shown how the USA and the Soviet Union drifted away from each other after 1945. Following such events as the Berlin Blockade, the Korean War and the Hungarian uprising, the Superpowers became rivals. The formation of NATO (see page 38) and the Warsaw Pact (see page 39) was an acknowledgement by the Superpowers that at some point in the future they might be involved in a war against each other.

By 1953 both the USA and the Soviet Union possessed hydrogen bombs. Both countries continued to develop more powerful nuclear weapons. On 1 March 1954, the USA tested its biggest ever hydrogen bomb. Its explosive power was the equivalent of fifteen million tons of TNT (trinitrotoluene).

Winston Churchill described the global situation as a 'balance of terror'.

There was some hope that the two Superpowers would slow down their arms development, but in 1957 the situation changed completely when a Soviet rocket launched *Sputnik*, a satellite which could orbit the earth in one and a half hours. The USA saw this launch as a military threat.

During the years 1957–59, the USA increased its spending on missiles by 20 per cent, and President Dwight Eisenhower founded the National Aeronautics and Space Administration (NASA). The Americans were concerned that the USSR was overtaking the USA in arms development. Therefore, the USA expanded its training programme for engineers and scientists. In addition, the US Air Force increased the number of B-52 bombers, and the US navy equipped some of its submarines with nuclear weapons. The USA also placed missile bases in some European countries.

Nevertheless, because of the technological developments in weaponry, both the Superpowers were able to reduce their **conventional** (non-nuclear) forces during the 1950s. Each Superpower expected the next war to be based on nuclear weapons. Source B shows how the armed forces of the USA and the Soviet Union had developed by 1961.

Source A: US and Soviet weaponry by 1961		
Weapon	**USA**	**Soviet Union**
Inter-continental ballistic missiles (**ICBM**)	63	50+
Submarine-launched ballistic missiles (**SLBM**)	96	0
Medium/ intermediate-range ballistic missiles (**MRBM/IRBM**)	90	200
Long-range bombers	600	190
Aircraft carriers	24	0
Nuclear submarines	21	2
Conventional submarines	174	428
Active military manpower	2,606,000	3,800,000

By 1961, relations between the Superpowers were rather strained. The U-2 crisis (see page 50) and events in Berlin during 1961 (see chapter 5) had quashed any hopes of improvements, but it was events close to the USA which almost brought the world to nuclear war.

Tasks

1. What did Churchill mean by the phrase 'balance of terror'?

2. Describe one way in which the USA developed its arms programme after 1957.

3. Study Source A. Which Superpower would consider itself the weaker of the two?

4. Briefly explain the key features of the arms race in the 1950s.

What were the causes of the Cuban Missiles Crisis?

UNITED STATES
Miami

Havana

CUBA

Bay of Pigs

N

0   200km

Guantánamo
Bay

Map of Cuba

Background to the crisis

The Cuban Missiles Crisis, which took place over a few days in October 1962, brought the Superpowers to the brink of nuclear war. Cuba had been a thorn in the side of the USA since 1959, when a revolution had brough Fidel Castro to power. Castro had ejected all US businesses and investment. In retaliation, the USA refused to buy Cuba's biggest export – sugar. The Soviet Union quickly saw a way to gain influence in the Caribbean. The Soviets offered to buy Cuban sugar and also to provide machinery, oil and technological assistance. Castro was now closely linked to the Soviet Union, and he professed that his political leanings were in the direction of communism.

Khrushchev, the leader of the Soviet Union, was keen to challenge the USA. He had been unable to re-unite Berlin but was sure that he could out-manoeuvre John F. Kennedy, the inexperienced new American president. Moreover, Khrushchev needed some successes to deflect criticisms of his failures within the Soviet Union.

OVER THE GARDEN WALL

Tasks

1. *Study Source A. What is its view of relations between the Superpowers?*

2. *Devise two captions for the cartoon – one from the viewpoint of Kennedy and one from that of Khrushchev.*

The Cuban Missiles Crisis

US involvement in the Bay of Pigs pushed Castro much closer to the Soviet Union. At the end of 1961, in a move which greatly concerned Kennedy and his advisors, the Cuban leader declared his conversion to communism.

By the end of 1961, there were Soviet military advisers and combat units stationed on the island. Khrushchev saw the move into Cuba as the beginnings of the spread of communism into Latin America. He was concerned by US missile bases in Italy and Turkey, and thus Soviet bases in Cuba would restore the balance of power. In addition, following the Bay of Pigs, he could claim to be defending Cuba from future attacks from the USA and disgruntled Cuban exiles.

Khrushchev continued to send military supplies to Cuba throughout 1962, and in September Soviet technicians began to install ballistic missiles. Khrushchev was able to say that any weapons were being sent in order to defend Cuba and were not offensive, unlike the missiles the USA had placed in Turkey. The situation suddenly changed on 14 October when a U2 spy plane took photographs of Cuba which showed that Soviet intermediate range missile bases were being constructed. It was estimated that the missiles would be operational by November. The Intermediate Range Ballistic Missiles (IRBM) could hit almost all US cities and therefore posed a serious threat to the country's security.

Source D: Stephen Ambrose, a US historian, writing in 1985, about the motives behind Khrushchev's decision to place nuclear weapons on Cuba

Khrushchev was frustrated in the nuclear field, unable to push the West out of Berlin, incapable of matching the US in Inter-Continental Ballistic Missiles (ICBMs), and increasingly irritated by Mao Zedong criticising Soviet weakness, began to look elsewhere for an opportunity to alter the strategic balance. He found it in Cuba.

Source E: The map shows the Soviet Union's military build up on Cuba in 1962 and the range of the nuclear missiles

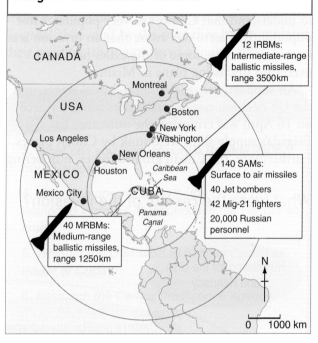

Tasks

11. *Look at Sources D and E. Why do you think that Cuba was attractive to the Soviet Union?*

12. *Draw a concept map, like the one below, to show the reasons behind Khrushchev's decision to place missiles on Cuba. Place the reasons clockwise in order of importance.*

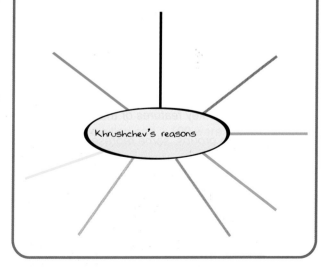

What were the key features of the crisis?

The period from when President Kennedy first saw the photographs of the missile bases to the Soviet decision to dismantle them lasted thirteen days. To the world it seemed much longer, and for the participants it must have seemed endless. When President Kennedy learned of the missiles, he set up a committee of twelve advisers, the closest of whom was his brother, Robert. The various options open to the USA were discussed – bomb Cuba and the Soviet Union using nuclear missiles; invade Cuba; use an air-strike to destroy the missile bases; blockade Cuba; or do nothing.

As the crisis mounted, certain military decisions were taken. It was decided to place a naval blockade (quarantine) around Cuba to prevent any Soviet ship delivering military materials. The blockade was to stretch 3300 kilometres around Cuba. A fleet of Polaris submarines was made ready for action and 156 ICBMs were made ready for combat. Furthermore, air-force bombers were in the air on patrol and hundreds of thousands of soldiers were placed on combat alert.

Source A: **Photograph of a missile site in Cuba taken from a U2 spy plane**

Source B: From President Kennedy's television address to the people of the USA, 22 October 1962

The transformation of Cuba into an important strategic base by the presence of long-range offensive weapons of mass destruction creates an explicit threat to the peace and security of all the Americas...

This sudden and secret decision to place strategic weapons outside of Soviet soil is a deliberately provocative and unjustified change in the existing state of affairs. Our objective must be to prevent the use of these missiles against the USA or any other country, and to secure their withdrawal or elimination from the western hemisphere...

We will not risk the costs of worldwide nuclear war in which the fruits of victory would be ashes in our mouth – but neither will we shrink from the risk at any time.

As Kennedy spoke on television, US armed forces prepared themselves for action. He informed Khrushchev that the Soviet convoy approaching Cuba would be stopped, and if any ship was found to be carrying offensive military equipment it would not be permitted to pass the blockade and would have to return to the Soviet Union.

Source C: An extract from Khrushchev's first letter to Kennedy, 27 October 1962

Your rockets are situated in Britain and Italy and are aimed at us. Your rockets are situated in Turkey. You are worried by Cuba. You say that it worries you because it is a distance of 90 miles from you, but Turkey is on our border.

Source D: A British cartoon about the Cuban Missiles Crisis, published in November 1962

Diary of Events

At the height of the crisis, issues had to be dealt with not only on a daily basis, but sometimes on an hourly one. The diary of events shows events over five days.

22 October:	Kennedy's television address
24 October:	18 Soviet ships approaching Cuba turned around to avoid confrontation with the US blockade (quarantine). Kennedy demanded the removal of all missiles and failure to do so would lead to the invasion of Cuba
26 October:	Khrushchev sent Kennedy a letter, offering to remove the missiles if the blockade was removed and there was a promise not to invade Cuba
27 October:	Khrushchev sent a tougher letter. He promised to remove the missiles if the USA removed its missiles from Turkey. U2 spy plane shot down over Cuba by Soviet missile. The crisis deepened
28 October:	President Kennedy, at the suggestion of his brother, decided to ignore the second letter and accepted the terms of the first. He added that if there was no positive Soviet response by 29 October, the US forces would invade Cuba. Khrushchev accepted the offer. The USA agreed to remove missiles from Turkey, but this would take place well after the removal of the missiles on Cuba.

Tasks

1. *Study Sources A (page 61) and B. How was President Kennedy able to justify his reaction to the activities of the Soviet Union?*

2. *Can you suggest reasons why President Kennedy took the unusual step of using the television to talk about the crisis?*

3. *Look at Source C. Do you think that Khrushchev had a valid argument for his decision to place the weapons on Cuba?*

4. *Look at Source D. what can you learn about the crisis from the source?*

What were the results of the crisis?

Kennedy seemed to have won the war of words and the perception was that Khrushchev had backed down. Many people saw Kennedy as a great statesman who had stood up to the communists. The deal over missiles in Turkey was not made public at the time. There were many leading politicians in the Soviet Union who thought Khrushchev had been humiliated and looked to remove him. Mao Zedong, the leader of China, criticised Khrushchev for placing the missiles in Cuba and then for backing down. Khrushchev saw the crisis as a victory for himself because he had saved Cuba from invasion and knew that the missiles in Turkey would be removed. Khrushchev was sacked in 1964.

> **Source A: From a speech by President Kennedy in June 1963. He was speaking about how the crisis had come to an end**
>
> *In the final analysis our most basic common link is the fact that we all inhabit this planet. We all breathe the same air. We all cherish our children's future. And we are all mortal.*

The Superpowers had almost gone to war – a war that would have destroyed much of the world. There was relief that the crisis was over and there was a great reduction of tension. To ensure that the two leaders did not have to communicate by letter in the case of a crisis, a hotline telephone link was established between the White House in Washington D.C. and the Kremlin in Moscow.

Further improvements came when the **Partial Test Ban Treaty** was signed in August 1963, whereby both the USA and Soviet Union agreed to stop testing nuclear weapons in the atmosphere. This was followed by the **Nuclear Non-proliferation Treaty** signed in 1968, which was designed to stop the spread of nuclear weapons. Those countries signing agreed not to develop nuclear weapons. The idea that the arms race had almost brought about nuclear war helped to push the Superpowers to consider limitations to their arsenals, and talks began in 1969. These became known as Strategic Arms Limitation Talks (see page 78), which became part of the policy of *détente*, a reduction in tension between the USA and Soviet Union.

Observers could see that relations had improved between the Superpowers in 1963 because the USA sold grain to the Soviet Union following poor harvests there. However, there were some in Europe who had taken exception to Kennedy acting on his own during the crisis. There had been little consultation with other countries and, in 1966, France withdrew from the military side of NATO (See page 38).

Tasks

1. What can you learn about President Kennedy from Source A?

2. Working in groups – one representing the government of the USA and one the government of the Soviet Union – prepare a speech which clearly supports your action during the crisis.

3. Write a letter addressed to Kennedy and Khrushchev explaining your feelings about their actions in the crisis.

4. Re-read the section on the Cuban Missiles Crisis (pages 57–63). Consider its effects and then copy and complete the table below.

Effects for Superpower relations	Effects for the world	Effects for Cuba	Effects for the Soviet Union	Effects for the USA

Examination practice

This section provides guidance on how to answer Question 4 on Paper 1, which is worth six marks.

Question 4 – six-mark question

Describe the key features of the Cuban Missiles Crisis.

You are offered a choice in Question 4: two similar questions, 4(a) and 4(b). You will have to show that you know quite a bit of factual information about your chosen topic, so choose carefully. Both usually start with the same words: 'Describe the key features of…'. With 6 marks, the event whose key features you have to describe is usually quite an important one.

How to answer

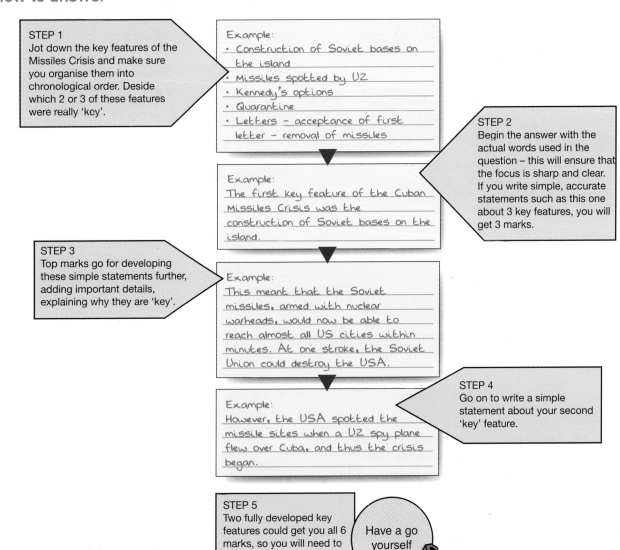

STEP 1
Jot down the key features of the Missiles Crisis and make sure you organise them into chronological order. Deside which 2 or 3 of these features were really 'key'.

Example:
• Construction of Soviet bases on the island
• Missiles spotted by U2
• Kennedy's options
• Quarantine
• Letters – acceptance of first letter – removal of missiles

STEP 2
Begin the answer with the actual words used in the question – this will ensure that the focus is sharp and clear. If you write simple, accurate statements such as this one about 3 key features, you will get 3 marks.

Example:
The first key feature of the Cuban Missiles Crisis was the construction of Soviet bases on the island.

STEP 3
Top marks go for developing these simple statements further, adding important details, explaining why they are 'key'.

Example:
This meant that the Soviet missiles, armed with nuclear warheads, would now be able to reach almost all US cities within minutes. At one stroke, the Soviet Union could destroy the USA.

STEP 4
Go on to write a simple statement about your second 'key' feature.

Example:
However, the USA spotted the missile sites when a U2 spy plane flew over Cuba, and thus the crisis began.

STEP 5
Two fully developed key features could get you all 6 marks, so you will need to write at least two good length paragraphs.

Have a go yourself

7 Czechoslovakia: the Prague Spring

Source A: Soviet troops posing with Czechoslovakian children in Prague, 1968

Source B: A Soviet tank surrounded by Czechoslovakian protesters, Prague, 1968

Tasks

Sources A and B show different reactions to the Soviet invasion of Czechoslovakia in 1968.

1. *In what ways are they different?*
2. *Why do you think they are different?*
3. *Devise a Soviet propaganda caption for each photograph.*

The Cuban Missiles Crisis of 1962 was the closest the Superpowers had come to nuclear war. However, this crisis was followed by a period of *détente,* a thawing in relations between the two sides in the Cold War. A hot line was set up between Washington and Moscow, and in 1963 the Superpowers signed a Partial Test Ban Treaty. The Soviet invasion of Czechoslovakia in 1968 severely tested *détente* and showed that the Soviet Union would not tolerate reforms which threatened their control of the buffer states of Eastern Europe.

This chapter answers the following questions:

- Why was there opposition to Soviet control of Czechoslovakia?
- What were the 'Prague Spring' reforms?
- Why did the Soviet Union re-establish control?
- What were the key features and consequences of the Soviet invasion?

Exam skills

This chapter gives guidance on how to answer Question 5 on Paper 1. This question is worth 15 marks. It gives you four events from across the whole period covered by this book and asks you to explain the importance of three of them, using your own knowledge.

Why was there opposition to Soviet control?

Since 1948 Czechoslovakia had, in many ways, been a 'model satellite'. The standard of living there was generally better than in other **satellite states**. Moreover, the Czechoslovakian government was obedient to the Soviet Union. However, in the 1960s opposition to Soviet control grew for several reasons.

Many remembered the actions of the Soviet Union in 1948 and the brutal murder of Jan Masaryk (see page 25). Antonin Novotny had been the Czech leader since 1957. He was unpopular because he was a hard-line communist who slavishly followed the Soviet line and refused to introduce reform. In addition Novotny was slow to follow Khrushchev's policy of **de-Stalinisation** (see page 40). He was especially slow to release political prisoners jailed under Stalin.

The Czechoslovakian economy was in serious decline in the 1960s, and this decline led to a fall in the standard of living. The Soviet Union forced Czechoslovakian industry to produce raw materials, such as steel, for the Soviet economy. Yet the Czechoslovakian economy needed those raw materials. The Soviet Union also stopped Czechoslovakian factories from producing consumer goods. In 1962–3 national income fell. Novotny's attempts at reform after 1965, known as the New Economic Model, were not successful, since they produced a surplus of consumer goods that few people could afford.

The failure of economic reform encouraged many Czechoslovakians to demand greater democracy. In October 1967 a number of reformers, including Alexander Dubcek and the economist Ota Sik, challenged Novotny's leadership at a meeting of the Central Committee of the Communist Party. In December Dubcek invited Leonid Brezhnev, the Soviet leader, to Prague. Brezhnev was surprised at the extent of opposition to Novotny. He withheld support for the Czechoslovakian leader.

On 5 January 1968, Novotny was replaced as First Secretary of the Communist Party (the top position in the party) by Alexander Dubcek, a move supported by Brezhnev. In March Novotny resigned as President of Czechoslovakia and was replaced by General Ludvik Svoboda. Svoboda, a

Biography Alexander Dubcek, 1921–1992

Alexander Dubcek was born in the Slovakian part of Czechoslovakia on 27 November 1921. During the Second World War, Dubcek was active as a communist **guerrilla** in opposition to the Nazi occupation. After the war he worked in a factory and served as secretary of local Communist committees. In the early 1950s he was appointed to the central committee, and by 1964 he had risen to the chairmanship of the Slovak Communist Party. He became more liberal in his views and began to support the idea of private enterprise.

Although he was a senior communist official, after 1964 Dubcek increasingly supported capitalist economic views that favoured a greater role for private enterprises. He also began to openly associate with intellectuals and artists. In 1967 he was supported by several interests in Czechoslovakia in securing the dismissal of the Czechoslovak Communist leader Novotny. The result was that Dubcek himself was appointed as First Secretary of the Czechoslovak Communist Party early in 1968. In 1989, after the collapse of the Soviet Union, Dubcek was invited to become leader of the Social Democratic Party, and he served for a time as speaker of the Czechoslovak parliament. Dubcek's influence on developments was cut short by his death in a car accident on November 7, 1992.

war hero whose name means 'freedom' in the Czech language, supported Dubcek's reform programme. Novotny had been removed from the two most powerful positions in the country.

Source A: From an interview with a worker in a locomotive factory in Prague in 1968

The Director told them they would produce 400 locomotives a year. They are making seventy. And go look at the scrapyard, at all the work that has been thrown out. They built a railway and then took it down again. Who's responsible for this? The Communist Party set up the system. We were robbed of our output, our wages.

Source B: From a speech given by Luvik Vaculik, a leading figure in the Czechoslovakian reform movement, in March 1968

In twenty years not one human problem has been solved in our country, from primary needs like flats, schools, to the more subtle needs such as fulfilling oneself, the need for people to trust one another, and the development of education. I feel that our Republic has lost its good reputation.

Source C: Czechoslovakian participants in a Youth and Student Festival in 1968 carry posters of Svoboda and Dubcek

Tasks

1. *What can you learn Sources A and B about the growth of opposition to communism in Czechoslovakia?*

2. *What does Source C suggest about attitudes to the two leaders at that time?*

What were the 'Prague Spring' reforms?

The 'Prague Spring' refers to a series of reforms introduced by Dubcek in the spring of 1968. The Czechs called it 'socialism with a human face'. Dubcek remained a devoted communist, but he wanted to win support for the communist regime by removing its worst features. The reforms included:

Greater political freedom, including free speech and the abolition of press censorship. By March 1968 the newspapers were printing uncensored discussions of political and social problems. The coverage of news by Czech radio and television became fuller. Corruption and bureaucratic delays were exposed by the media. Communist party leaders were 'grilled' on live television.

A reduction in the powers of the secret police to imprison without trial.

The removal of travel restrictions and fresh contact with the West, such as trade with West Germany.

Dubcek meets Czechoslovakians

A ten-year programme for political change which would bring about democratic elections, a multi-party state and create a new form of democratic socialism. In other words, giving the people of Czechoslovakia a greater say in the running of the country.

The creation of works councils representing the workforce to improve working conditions in factories and an increase in rights for members of trade unions.

Dubcek's reforms, however, encouraged opponents of communism and led to demands for even more radical reforms. For example, in June 1968 the Social Democrats began to form a separate party as a rival to the Communist Party. Around the same time Ludvik Vaculik, a leading journalist, published a manifesto entitled *The Two Thousand Words*. In it he called on the Czechoslovakian people to take the initiative and force even more extreme reform.

The Soviet Union was suspicious of the changes taking place in Czechoslovakia for several reasons. Czechoslovakia was one of the most important countries in the Warsaw Pact. It was centrally placed (see map page 38) and had the strongest industry. Brezhnev was worried that Czechoslovakia might leave the Warsaw Pact, allowing NATO to move in. This outcome would split the Eastern bloc into two and advance NATO's frontier 700 km further to the east so that it bordered the Soviet Union itself.

Tasks

1. *What was meant by the 'Prague Spring?'*

2. *Describe one decision taken by Dubcek during the Prague Spring.*

Why did the Soviet Union re-establish control?

The Soviets were also worried that the new ideas in Czechoslovakia might spread to other countries in Eastern Europe. Brezhnev came under pressure from the East German leader, Walter Ulbricht, and the Polish leader, Gomulka, to stop reform in Czechoslovakia.

Furthermore, the Soviet Union was afraid that Czechoslovakia was becoming closer to West Germany. It seemed to them that industrial relations between the Czechs and West Germans were being strengthened from day to day. Eventually West Germany might come to dominate the economy of Czechoslovakia and other countries in Eastern Europe.

The Soviet invasion followed the build up of tension between the Warsaw Pact countries led by the Soviet Union and the Czechoslovak government of Dubcek.

Source A: From a letter sent by the Soviet leadership to the Czech Communist Party

Developments in your country are causing deep anxiety among us. We cannot agree to have hostile forces push your country away from the road of communism. This is something more than your own concern. It is the common concern of our countries, which have joined in the Warsaw Treaty...

Tasks

1. *What reasons are suggested in Source A for Soviet concerns over Czechoslovakia?*

2. *Write a brief reply from Dubcek to this letter. Remember, he will be trying to defend his reforms and yet remove Soviet fears.*

DATE (1968)	EVENT
June	
	Soviet tanks remained in Czechoslovakia after Warsaw Pact military exercises
July	
	Brezhnev met with leaders of the Warsaw Pact countries in Warsaw. They shared his concerns over events in Prague
	A few days later Brezhnev met with Dubcek. Dubcek agreed not to allow a new Social Democratic Party and to remain in the Warsaw Pact. However, he insisted on going ahead with his reform programme. The Soviet Union seemed reassured, and tension eased
August	
3 August	Brezhnev and representatives from Warsaw Pact countries met with Dubcek in Bratislava and signed the Bratislava Declaration declaring their faith in communism. Once again, Brezhnev seemed reassured
	The leader of Yugoslavia, Tito, who was distrusted by the Soviet Union, was given an enthusiastic reception in Czechoslovakia during a visit in late July. It seemed yet again that Dubcek was moving towards independence from the Soviet Union
15–18 August	Three day meeting session of the Soviet **Politburo** to decide what action to take. Brezhnev spoke to Dubcek on the phone, shouting at him that his actions in Prague would bring down the Warsaw Pact
20 August	The Soviet Union invaded Czechoslovakia

What were the key features and consequences of the Soviet invasion?

Source A: A Prague radio report, 21 August 1968

Yesterday troops from the Soviet Union crossed the frontiers of the Czechoslovakian Socialist Republic. This happened without the knowledge of the President of the Republic or the First Secretary of the Czechoslovak Communist Party Central Committee. The Czechoslovak Communist Party regard this act as contrary to basic principles of good relations between communist states.

Source B: A Soviet news agency report, 21 August 1968

The party and government of the Czechoslovak Socialist Republic have asked the Soviet Union and other allies to give the Czechoslovak people urgent assistance including assistance with armed forces. This request was brought about by the threat from counter-revolutionary forces working with foreign forces hostile to communism.

On 20–21 August 1968, hundreds and thousands of Soviet troops, backed by units from Bulgaria, East Germany, Hungary and Poland, entered Czechoslovakia. Czechoslovakians threw petrol bombs at the Soviet tanks as they moved through Prague. Buildings were set on fire, and protestors assembled in Wenceslas Square. Barricades were set up in the streets. Students tore down street names to confuse the invaders. Some students even climbed onto the tanks and tried to argue with the Soviet soldiers. Anti-Soviet broadcasters stayed on the air by moving from one hiding place to another. However, there was no armed resistance by the Czechoslovakian army, and fewer than a hundred people were killed.

Dubcek and the other leaders were arrested and taken to Moscow, where they were forced to accept the end of Czechoslovakian moves towards democracy. Over the next few years, hard-line Czechoslovakian officials replaced the reforming Czechoslovakian leaders.

Source C: Prague residents surround a Soviet tank on Wenceslas Square during confrontations between demonstrators and the Warsaw Pact troops and tanks

Consequences of the invasion

The Soviet invasion had important consequences for Czechoslovakia, the Soviet Union, the Warsaw Pact and the Cold War.

Czechoslovakia

Demonstrations against the Soviet invasion went on until April 1969. In January 1969 Jan Palach, a student, set fire to himself in Wenceslas Square in protest against the Soviet invasion. Nevertheless the Czech Communist Party was purged. Dubcek was forced to resign. Under his replacement, Gustav Husak, Czechoslovakia reverted to strict communist rule. Dubcek was not executed but was sent as ambassador to Turkey and then forced to resign from the Czech Communist Party.

Source E: The funeral in Prague of the student Jan Palach, who became a symbol of anti-Soviet resistance in Europe

Tasks

1. a) What differences are there between Sources A and B in their views about the invasion of Czechoslovakia?

   b) Why do they give different views?

2. Produce two sets of headlines for the day after the invasion for:
   - A Soviet newspaper
   - A Czechoslovakian newspaper

3. Do you think the actions of Vasil Bilak justify the Soviet invasion? Explain your answer.

4. Briefly explain the key features of the Soviet invasion of Czechoslovakia in 1968.

5. Devise two captions for Sources C and D for:
   - A Soviet newspaper
   - A Czechoslovakian newspaper

6. Source E was published in national Czechoslovakian newspapers. Devise a suitable caption for the photo.

Soviet Union

The invasion of Czechoslovakia gave rise to the **Brezhnev Doctrine**. This doctrine redefined communism as a one-party system and declared that all member countries had to remain part of the Warsaw Pact. The invasion also sent out a message to the members of the Warsaw Pact that the Soviet Union would suppress any attempt to relax communist control.

Warsaw Pact

On the other hand, some Communist countries began to move away from Moscow. President Ceausescu of Romania refused to send troops to join the forces invading Czechoslovakia and took an increasingly independent line against the Soviet Union. Albania did the same and left the Warsaw Pact for good in 1968. The Soviet Union did not react because it was preoccupied with events in Czechoslovakia.

Cold War

The Soviet invasion temporarily worsened relations between East and West. Western countries, especially Britain and the USA, protested about Soviet actions. However, the invasion did not ultimately not endanger Soviet-American relations, and *détente* continued after a slight break (see page 76). The USA was in the middle of a presidential election during 1968 and was also pre-occupied with the **Vietnam War**. To a degree, the events in Czechoslovakia took the pressure off the USA because many other countries in the West condemned the Soviet Union's actions. However, in another way, the war in Vietnam allowed the Soviet Union to move into Czechoslovakia with impunity because it knew the USA would do nothing.

However, the invasion of Czechoslovakia did increase the rivalry between China and the Soviet Union. China criticised the use of force against a fellow communist nation. The Chinese feared that the Soviet Union might take the same action against China.

> **Source F: The Brezhnev Doctrine, 1968**
>
> *When internal and external forces hostile to socialism attempt to turn the development of any communist country in the direction of the capitalist system, when a threat arises to the cause of communism in that country, a threat to the communist commonwealth as a whole – it becomes not only a problem for the people of that country but also a general problem, the concern of all communist countries.*

Tasks

7. Study Source F. What implications does the Brezhnev Doctrine have for all countries in the Warsaw Pact?

8. Prioritise the consequences of the Soviet invasion, beginning with the most important. Give a reason for your decision.

9. Make a copy of the table below.

	Causes	Events
Similarities		
Differences		

Use the table to compare the Hungarian uprising of 1956 (see pages 41–47) with the events in Czechoslovakia in 1968. One example has been done for you.

10. What is the greatest difference between the two events?

Examination practice

This section provides guidance on how to answer Question 5 on Paper 1, which is worth 15 marks.

This question is really three shorter questions on events which are all related to a big theme from across the Unit as a whole, such as 'international relations' or 'the Cold War'.

You have a limited choice: four events are listed and you have to write about three of them.

Question 5 – 15-mark question

Explain the importance of **three** of the following in the Cold War:
- The Berlin Airlift, 1948–9
- The Warsaw Pact, 1955
- The Prague Spring, 1968
- The Helsinki Agreements, 1975

Each of the three items you choose from the list of four will be marked out of 5. Let's see how to get full marks on The Prague Spring.

This is fine, but doesn't say how all this relates to the Cold War.

> **Answer 1**
> The Prague Spring was a reform movement in communist-controlled Czechoslovakia, led by Alexander Dubcek. There was more free discussion in the media, removal of travel restrictions, more rights for workers and proposals to bring in a more capitalist economy.

This is getting better, but only states that the crushing of the Prague Spring was important, it doesn't explain why it was.

> **Answer 2**
> The Prague Spring was a reform movement in communist-controlled Czechoslovakia, in the spring of 1968, led by Alexander Dubcek. There was more free discussion in the media, removal of travel restrictions, more rights for workers and proposals to bring in a more capitalist economy.
> It was important because Soviet leader Brezhnev sent in tanks to crush the reform movement.

Now we have a good length paragraph, explaining why the events of the Prague Spring were important in the history of the Cold War.

> **Answer 3**
> The Prague Spring was a reform movement in communist-controlled Czechoslovakia, in the spring of 1968, led by Alexander Dubcek. There was more free discussion in the media, removal of travel restrictions, more rights for workers, proposals to bring in a more capitalist economy, a multi-party democracy, perhaps even to leave the Warsaw Pact.
> It was important because Soviet leader Brezhnev sent in tanks to crush the reform movement. His action showed that the Soviet Union was not going to allow any members of the Warsaw Pact to leave the alliance, or to develop multi-party democracy. This was called 'The Brezhnev Doctrine'. Britain and the USA complained about the Soviet action and détente was halted for a while. The division between east and west, communist and capitalist, which was at the heart of the Cold War continued for another 20 years.

In the examination you would go on to do the same thing for two more events from the three remaining items in the question. Have a go at completing the answer to this question, by choosing two more events.

Have a go yourself

3 Why did the Cold War end? From *détente* (1972) to the collapse of the Soviet Union (1991)

Source A: From a speech by President Reagan to the British parliament, June 1982

From Stettin on the Baltic to Varna on the Black Sea, the regimes planted by totalitarianism have had more than thirty years to establish their legitimacy. But none – not one regime – has yet been able to risk free elections. Regimes planted by bayonets do not take root... If history teaches anything, it teaches self-delusion in the face of unpleasant facts is folly... US military strength is a prerequisite to peace, but let it be clear we maintain this strength in the hope it will never be used, for the ultimate determinant in the struggle that is now going on in the world will not be bombs and rockets but a test of wills and ideas, a trial of spiritual resolve, the values we hold, the beliefs we cherish, the ideals to which we are dedicated.

Task

What can you learn from Source A about President Reagan's attitude to the Soviet Union and its **satellite states**?

There was some hope at the end of the 1960s that relations between the USA and the Soviet Union would substantially improve. In the 1970s, SALT and the Helsinki Agreements had brought about distinct changes, but the Soviet Union's invasion of Afghanistan in 1979 plunged the world into what became known as the Second Cold War. Relations between the Superpowers in the early 1980s were as cold as they had ever been – yet by 1989 the leaders of the USA and the Soviet Union had announced that the Cold War was over.

Each chapter within this section explains a key issue and examines important lines of enquiry as outlined below.

Détente and its collapse

Source A: From 'Basic principles of relations between the USSR and the USA', signed in Moscow, 29 May 1972

The USSR and the USA have agreed that differences in ideology are not obstacles to the bilateral development of normal relations based on the principles of sovereignty, equality, non-interference in internal affairs and mutual advantage. The USSR and USA will do their utmost to avoid military confrontations and to prevent the outbreak of nuclear war. The USSR and USA have a special responsibility to do everything in their power so that conflicts will not arise which would increase international tensions.

Task

In what ways does Source A show that relations between the USA and Soviet Union (USSR) had improved after the Cuban Missiles Crisis?

Chapter 6 covered the improvement in relations between the USA and Soviet Union in the years after the Cuban Missiles Crisis. The change in relations became known as *détente* – a French word that refers to a reduction in the tension between the Superpowers. The lack of real threats to world peace during the **Vietnam War** and the Soviet invasion of Czechoslovakia were evidence of this easing of tension. Attempts at arms limitation, summit talks and personal visits all seemed to indicate that there was good reason for optimism.

However, despite high points, such as the Strategic Arms Limitation Treaty (SALT) in 1972 and the Human Rights Agreements at Helsinki in 1975, the Cold War never quite went away. The Soviet invasion of Afghanistan in 1979 seemed to indicate that the threat of a 'hot' conflict between the Superpowers remained a possibility. Following the invasion, it was said that a second Cold War had started.

This chapter answers the following questions:

• How did *détente* develop after the Cuban Missiles Crisis?
• What were the key features of SALT I?
• How important were the Helsinki Agreements?
• Why did the Soviet Union invade Afghanistan in 1979?
• What were the immediate effects of the invasion?

How did *détente* develop after the Cuban Missiles Crisis?

After the Cuban Missiles Crisis (see Chapter 6), there was a move to improve relations and relax tension between the USA and Soviet Union which became known as *détente*. The threat of nuclear war had had a sobering effect on all concerned, and the attempts to maintain sound relations was always evident in the 1960s in spite of new and emerging crises. The hotline between Washington and the Kremlin improved the speed of communications and the Test Ban Treaty (see page 63) showed a willingness to look at the issue of developing nuclear weapons.

The new leader of the Soviet Union, Leonid Brezhnev, had put forward his view of Soviet foreign policy when he took over from Khrushchev. He stated that if a capitalist country threatened any **communist** country then other communist states had to intervene by using force. By 1968, this had become known as the Brezhnev Doctrine (see page 72).

The widening of the Cold War

However, the Cold War continued, especially in the Middle East. After the Israeli victory in the **Six Day War of 1967**, Arab states were drawn more closely towards the Soviet Union because the USA had supplied so much military hardware to Israel. Each of the Superpowers supplied arms to the warring sides in the Middle East but actual relations between the USA and the Soviet Union did not ever match those at the time of Cuba. Nor did the Soviet invasion of Czechoslovakia in August 1968 (see Chapter 7) endanger Soviet-American relations.

In its quest to halt the spread of communism, the USA had sent military advisers to South Vietnam in the 1950s and had then sent troops in 1965. However, the war in Vietnam had not gone well for the USA. Despite a huge military presence, it could not defeat the North Vietnamese and the Vietcong (a derogatory term used to describe Vietnamese communists). By 1968 the USA was seeking to end the war, and peace talks began in the spring of 1968. After Nixon became president, it was hoped that if the USA improved trade and technology links and made an offer of arms reduction, then Brezhnev might persuade his North Vietnamese ally to negotiate an end to the war. The idea of offering concessions was called 'linkage' by Nixon's advisers.

Tasks

1. *Look back at pages 27–28 and re-read the section on the **Truman Doctrine**. Compare the Truman and Brezhnev Doctrines. For example, why were they formed? What were the key features of each? Did they change relations between the USA and Soviet Union?*

2. *Describe one reason why Brezhnev issued his Doctrine.*

3. *Describe one way in which* détente *developed in the 1960s.*

Source A: **Nixon (right) and Brezhnev (left) meeting in Moscow in 1974**

Nixon visited Moscow in 1972 and he made it clear that he did not see Vietnam as an obstacle to the process of *détente* even though the Soviet Union was supplying arms to North Vietnam. Nixon had visited China three months earlier, and Brezhnev did not want to see a Chinese–US alliance develop. The Soviet leader was keen to gain access to US technology and further grain sales, so both the Superpower leaders had their own motives for seeking improved relations.

At the meeting, Nixon agreed to take part in a European Security Conference, from which emerged the Helsinki Agreements (see pages 82–83).

Brezhnev played the part of intermediary between Washington and Hanoi (capital of North Vietnam), and peace between the USA and North Vietnam was eventually signed in 1973. This was remarkable because, only eleven years before, the Superpowers had almost been at war themselves.

Source C: Photograph of the Ho Chi Minh Trail. The Vietcong were assisted by Soviets and Chinese along this jungle supply route

Source B: Table of US casualties in the Vietnam War during the years 1966–70. By 1968 the USA had more than 500,000 troops in South Vietnam. President Nixon began to reduce numbers the following year.

Year	Killed in action	Wounded in action	Missing in action
1966	5,008	29,992	61
1967	9,378	56,013	113
1968	14,594	87,388	176
1969	9,414	53,390	112
1970	4,221	24,835	101

Tasks

4. *Look at Source B. Explain why President Nixon wanted to end US involvement in Vietnam.*

5. *What can you learn about the attitude of the North Vietnamese and Vietcong from Source C?*

6. *What was meant by the term 'linkage'?*

7. *Explain why linkage was important to the USA and Soviet Union.*

What were the key features of SALT I?

Early in Nixon's presidency, a decision was made to talk about **nuclear weapons**. The move to *détente* and the idea of linkage, together with economic problems in the Soviet Union, made the idea of some attempt to limit the arms race quite attractive.

Talks held in Helsinki and Vienna over a period of almost three years produced the first accords (SALT I) in May 1972.

SALT I was seen as the first step in a long journey to reaching very positive goals, but the fact that **strategic bombers** were not limited and there were no restrictions on developing new weapons did disappoint those campaigning for a safer world.

Agreements

- Anti-Ballistic Missile Treaty (**ABM**) – ABM systems allowed at only two sites, each site containing 100 missiles. The treaty was seen by many as a key piece in nuclear arms control because it was a clear recognition of the need to protect the nuclear balance by ensuring neither side could ever consider itself immune from retaliation.
- Interim Agreement on Offensive Arms – this imposed a five-year freeze on the total number of **ICBM** and **SLBM** launchers.
- Strategic bombers and their bombs not limited.
- No restriction on **MIRVs** (multiple independently targetable re-entry vehicles).
- Each side was allowed to use satellites to check that the other was not breaking the arms limits.

Source A: **Brezhnev (left) and Nixon (right) at the SALT I in 1972**

The Middle East and *détente*

The optimism of 1972 was put to the test in October 1973 during the Arab-Israeli War (Yom Kippur War). Syria and Egypt (armed and supplied by the Soviet Union) made surprise attacks on Israel (armed and supplied by the USA). After the Israelis had recovered from the surprise attacks, they regained the initiative and were sent replacement military equipment on the orders of President Nixon.

Tasks

1. *What can you say about the nature of SALT I agreement by looking at Source A?*

2. *Briefly explain the key features of the SALT Treaty.*

3. *Study Source B. Why was the development of MIRVs important in the arms race?*

4. *Draw a table to show why the USA and the Soviet Union wanted SALT and* détente. *Below are three reasons to start you off:*

USA's reasons	Soviet Union's reasons	Good for both reasons
Good relations with China	Reduce arms spending	Continue peaceful co-existence

Source B: Photograph showing the testing of a MIRV. Each line represents the path of a warhead that, if it were live, would detonate with the explosive power of 25 of the bombs dropped on Hiroshima

Source C: A cartoon about the role of the Superpowers in the Yom Kippur War published in *The Guardian* newspaper, 1973. Nixon is on the left and Brezhnev on the right. The soldiers in the middle represent the Arabs and Israelis

Tasks

5. *Study Source C. What message is the cartoonist trying to put across about the actions of Nixon and Brezhnev?*

6. *In what ways is the cartoon a depiction of the Cold War?*

Brezhnev put forward a plan: a joint USA–Soviet Union force would be on hand to save the Egyptian army from the Israelis. If the USA refused, then Soviet forces would go separately. Nixon did not want to accept the offer and was angry at Brezhnev's suggestion of independent action. Nixon put all US forces, including nuclear strike groups, on alert.

As an alternative, the USA suggested that a UN peacekeeping force of non-nuclear countries intervene in the conflict. Brezhnev accepted this proposal, and the Yom Kippur War ended with a ceasefire on 24 October 1973.

Nixon's visit to Moscow

Though relations were not warm, Nixon visited Brezhnev in Moscow in July 1974. After the meeting, the two leaders agreed:

- they would continue to remove the danger of war, particularly war involving nuclear and other weapons of mass destruction.
- to limit and eventually end the arms race, especially in **strategic warheads**. The two leaders said their ultimate objective was complete disarmament, which would be monitored by appropriate international control.
- they would contribute to the elimination of sources of international tension and military conflict.
- to relax tensions throughout the world.
- to develop broad, mutually beneficial co-operation in commercial, economic, scientific, technical and cultural fields. The aim was promoting increased understanding and confidence between the peoples of both countries.

Source D: Quote by the US historian S. Ambrose written in 1985

*SALT I in 1972 froze ICBM **deployment** but not MIRV, which was about as meaningful as freezing the cavalry of European countries in 1938 but not the tanks. Throughout the Nixon administration the USA added three warheads each day to the MIRV arsenal. It was a strange way to control the arms race.*

Space link-up

There were some encouraging consequences of the Moscow meeting. On 17 July 1975, three US astronauts and two Soviet cosmonauts met up in space. There was a symbolic handshake in space between the two sides and, along with sporting and cultural alliances, relations did seem to be on the mend.

Source E: Photograph of the Apollo-Soyuz crew space mission, 1975

Source F: From a speech by Secretary Brezhnev in 1975. He was talking about the importance of the space link-up

The flight was of historic significance because it was a symbol of the process of easing the international tension and also of the improvement of US-Soviet relations on the basis of peaceful co-existence. It was a practical contribution between the USA and the Soviet Union in the interests of world peace.

Source G: The badge worn by the US crew who took part in the Apollo-Soyuz space link-up in July 1975

Tasks

7. *What can you learn about the SALT agreements from Source D?*

8. *Study Sources E, F and G. Explain why the Apollo-Soyuz space mission was important for détente.*

9. *Describe one way in which US–Soviet relations changed in the early 1970s.*

How important were the Helsinki Agreements?

After Nixon and Brezhnev's meeting in July 1974, there were continuing attempts to keep *détente* developing. The Helsinki Agreements of 1975 were a product of this. The USA and the Soviet Union, along with 33 other nations, made declarations about three distinct international issues (called 'baskets' by the signatories).

SECURITY

Recognition of Europe's frontiers. Soviet Union accepted the existence of West Germany.

CO-OPERATION

There was a call for closer economic, scientific and cultural links – these would lead to even closer political agreement.

HUMAN RIGHTS

Each signatory agreed to respect human rights and basic freedoms such as thought, speech, religion and freedom from unfair arrest.

Source A: Front row, from left to right: Kissinger (Secretary of State, USA), Brezhnev, President Ford and Gromyko (Foreign Secretary, Soviet Union) at the signing of the Helsinki Agreements, 1 August 1975

Source B: From a speech by Brezhnev in Helsinki, 31 July 1975

No one should try . . . to dictate to other peoples how they should manage their internal affairs. It is only the people of each given state, and no one else, who have the right to decide their own internal affairs.

Tasks

1. *Look at the content of the first basket. Why could this be seen as a high-point of* détente?

2. *Look at the content of the second basket. In what ways would closer links bring political agreement?*

3. *What can you learn from Source B about Brezhnev's attitude to the agreements on human rights?*

4. *Why do you think Brezhnev was prepared to agree to 'basket three'?*

Superpower relations after Helsinki

SALT II

There was a commitment to arms limitations throughout the 1970s, even though the two Superpowers were competing in the Middle East, Latin America and Africa. SALT II began in 1974 and the treaty was signed in June 1979. After 1977, the new US President Carter was keen to link the issue of human rights to arms limitation as a way to put pressure on the Soviet Union. Following the human rights agreement at Helsinki in 1975, he sent a letter to the Soviet **dissident**, Andrei Sakharov, supporting the stand he and others were taking against Soviet authorities.

Carter's actions were seen as a gross interference in Soviet internal affairs, and Brezhnev made this clear in a speech during the Helsinki talks. In response, various groups were set up in eastern Europe, known as the Helsinki Groups, to monitor the Soviet Union's adherence to the Agreements. They, along with President Carter and other Human Rights organisations, complained about Soviet violations of the 1975 agreements. The violations that were highlighted covered lack of free speech, religious restrictions and lack of freedom of movement. The human rights issue was becoming an embarrassment for Brezhnev.

In spite of differences over human rights and Soviet interference in African states, talks on arms limitation continued. The Soviet Union was seen to be interfering in several African states and Carter asked for an increase in the defence budget in late 1978. Final agreements for SALT II were reached in June 1979. The terms were:

- A limit of 2400 strategic nuclear delivery vehicles (ICBMs, SLBMs, and heavy bombers) for each side.
- 1320 limit on MIRV systems for each side.
- A ban on construction of new land-based ICBM launchers.
- Limits on deployment of new types of strategic offensive arms.
- SALT II would last until 1985.

Worsening relations

Ratification of the treaty did not take place. The US **Congress** did not believe that the limits put forward in SALT II could be verified, and there was renewed concern over the 2000 Soviet troops stationed in Cuba. In late 1979, NATO decided to place long-range missiles in Europe. *Détente* was under pressure, but its end came unexpectedly when the Soviet Union invaded Afghanistan on 25 December 1979. The US **Senate** refused to ratify SALT II and many said that a second Cold War was starting.

> **Source C: The increase in missiles and warheads owned by the superpowers in the 1970s**

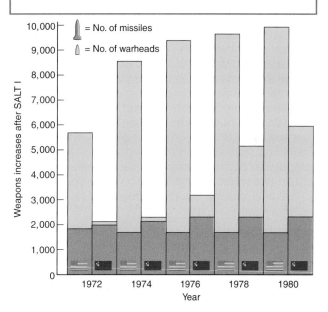

Tasks

1. *Can you suggest reasons why the issue of human rights was an 'embarrassment' for Brezhnev?*

2. *Study Source C. What can you learn about the increase in weapons owned by the Superpowers in the 1970s?*

3. *What do you think was meant by the term 'a second Cold War'?*

4. *Look back at this chapter and note down the successes and failures of détente. Then list its successes and failures in a table OR represent the successes/failures as a set of scales. Which side outweighs the other?*

Why did the Soviet Union invade Afghanistan in 1979?

Source A: From an article by the Soviet journalist Alexander Bovin in the Soviet newspaper *Izvestia*, April 1980. Bovin was explaining the reason for Soviet intervention in Afghanistan

We had to make a choice: we either had to bring in troops or let the Afghan communist revolution be defeated... It was not a simple decision to take. We knew that if the revolution failed it would pave the way for massive US presence in a country that borders on the Soviet Union and that this was a challenge to our country's security... We knew that we would have ceased to be a great power if we refrained from carrying the burden of taking unpopular but necessary decisions. There are situations when non-intervention is a disgrace and a betrayal. Such a situation developed in Afghanistan.

Source B: Map showing the geographical importance of Afghanistan

Background to the invasion

On 27 April 1978 the People's Democratic Party of Afghanistan (PDPA, a communist party) overthrew the government of Afghanistan. Nur Muhammad Taraki, Secretary General of the PDPA, became President of the Revolutionary Council and Prime Minister of the newly established Democratic Republic of Afghanistan. During its first eighteen months of rule, the PDPA imposed a communist-style reform programme. Decrees forcing changes in marriage customs and land reform were misunderstood by virtually all Afghans. In addition, thousands of members of the traditional élite – the Muslim religious establishment and intellectuals – were imprisoned, tortured or murdered.

The issue of Islamic fundamentalism

In September 1979 Hafizullah Amin, the Deputy Prime Minister, seized power from Taraki, but there was continued instability in the country because of the anti-Muslim policies. Thousands of Afghan Muslims joined the *mujahideen* – a **guerrilla** movement which proclaimed to be on a holy mission for Allah. They wanted to overthrow the Amin government. The *mujahideen* declared a *jihad* – a holy war – on the supporters of Amin. The Soviet military assistance programme, which had begun in 1978, was increased, and Amin's regime became dependent on Soviet military equipment and advisers. However, Amin did not

Tasks

1. *Study Source A. What can you learn about the reasons for the Soviet invasion of Afghanistan in 1979?*

2. *Study Source B. Make a list of the reasons why Afghanistan was important to each Superpower.*

wish to become too reliant on the Soviet Union and wanted to improve links with the USA. Unrest and chaos continued to grow in Afghanistan.

Brezhnev was concerned about the growing power and spread of **Islamic fundamentalism** and wanted to show the 30 million Muslims in the Soviet Union that there would be no changes to the way the Soviet Union was run. The Soviet Union saw fundamentalism as a great threat to the Soviet system.

The invasion

Between 25 December 1979 and 1 January 1980, more than 50,000 Soviet troops were sent to Afghanistan to restore order and protect the PDPA from the *mujahideen*. Brezhnev said the Soviet Union was only complying with the 1978 Treaty of Friendship, Co-operation and Good Neighbourliness that former President Taraki had signed.

On 27 December 1979, Amin was shot and replaced by Babrak Kamal, who had been in exile in Moscow. His position as head of the Afghan government depended entirely on Soviet military support. Many Afghan soldiers deserted to join the *mujahideen* and the Kamal government then required 85,000 Soviet soldiers to keep it in power.

Source C: Soviet troops and tanks in Afghanistan in 1980

Source D: From the hotline telephone conversation between Brezhnev and Carter on 28 December 1979. Brezhnev was telling Carter why Soviet forces had entered Afghanistan

We have been invited in by the Afghanistan government to protect it from some outside threat ... we shall remove our forces as soon as the situation stabilises.

Source E: From a newspaper article in the Chinese newspaper, *Beijing People's Daily* on 1 January 1980. It was discussing the Soviet invasion of Afghanistan

The invasion is a stepping-stone for a southward thrust towards Pakistan and India. There will be no peace in Southern Asia with Soviet soldiers in strategic Afghanistan.

Tasks

3. *Explain why some Afghan people opposed the governments of Taraki and Amin.*

4. *Work in groups to answer the following questions. You will need to think about issues such as Soviet foreign policy and Soviet ideas about control of people.*

   a) *Why do you think that the Soviet Union was prepared to send military equipment and advisers to Afghanistan?*

   b) *Why was Islamic fundamentalism a threat to the Soviet system?*

5. *Look at Source D. What is meant by the term 'hotline'?*

6. *How do you know that the invasion was a serious international crisis? Refer to the sources in your answer.*

7. *Briefly explain the key features of the Soviet invasion of Afghanistan.*

8. *Construct a concept map to show the reasons why the Soviet Union invaded Afghanistan.*

What were the immediate effects of the invasion?

President Carter was already under pressure in November 1979 following the seizure of US embassy staff as hostages in Iran. Carter had failed to solve that problem by the end of the year, and some in the USA were accusing him of being a weak leader. He therefore began to take a firm approach with the Soviet Union over the invasion. This became known as the **Carter Doctrine.** It was a policy that stated that the USA would use military force if necessary to defend its national interests in the Persian Gulf region (see map on page 84).

Source A: From President Carter's State of the Union speech (annual address by the president to the country) on 23 January 1980

Let our position be absolutely clear: an attempt by any outside force to gain control of the Persian Gulf region will be regarded as an assault on the vital interests of the United States of America, and such an assault will be repelled by any means necessary, including military force.

The Carter Doctrine also promised US military aid to all of the countries bordering Afghanistan. To carry out this policy Carter proposed the creation of a quick-strike military force that could intervene anywhere in the world at short notice (Rapid Deployment Force). He also called for a **draft** registration of 18–20-year-old men and for Congress to allow the **CIA** to increase its intelligence gathering activities.

The tough line was continued when President Carter asked the Senate to delay passing the SALT II treaty. The USA then cancelled all shipments of grain to the Soviet Union and US companies were forbidden to sell high technology there, such as computers and oil drilling equipment. It was also decided that assistance would be given to the guerrillas – *mujahideen* – who fought against the Soviet invaders.

Détente was dead by the beginning of 1980.

Source B: From an article in *Pravda*, the official Soviet newspaper, January 1980

Secretary Brezhnev has said that a mountain of lies has built up around the events of the invasion of Afghanistan. It is clear that an anti-Soviet campaign is being mounted. The USA is an absolutely unreliable partner, whose leadership is capable – at any moment – of cancelling treaties and agreements.

President Carter's most controversial decision after the Soviet invasion was to pressure the United States Olympic Committee to boycott the Moscow Olympic Games. Carter threatened to withhold funding and remove tax benefits. USOC agreed, and 61 other countries followed the USA's example. Thus international Superpower politics intruded into the Olympics. The sour relations which existed at the beginning of 1980 worsened at these Olympics. Some of those who boycotted the games held an alternative event called the 'Liberty Bell Classic'. At the official games, the Soviet Union won 195 medals, including 80 golds.

Tasks

1. *What is meant by the Carter Doctrine?*

2. *In what ways is the Carter Doctrine similar to the Truman Doctrine?*

3. *What was the reaction of President Carter to the invasion of Afghanistan? Construct a table as follows:*

Military reaction	Economic reaction	Political reaction

4. *Briefly explain the key features of relations between the USA and Soviet Union in the years 1972–79.*

9 Reagan and the 'Second Cold War'

Source A: Part of an article from *Pravda*, 23 December 1979. *Pravda* was the official newspaper of the Soviet Communist Party

Soviet–Afghan relations are based on a firm foundation of friendship and non-interference in each other's internal affairs. These relations have strengthened since April 1978, when power in Afghanistan shifted to the hands of the people. However, the CIA has been directly involved in training Afghan rebels in Pakistan, and maintains contacts with them in Afghanistan. CIA agents are operating in the Afghan-Pakistani border, some of them using the Drug Enforcement Administration as cover. The subversive anti-Afghan activities of US and other intelligence and sabotage services are a flagrant intervention in the internal affairs of Afghanistan. US and Chinese propaganda cannot camouflage these dangerous intrigues.

Tasks

1. *Read Source A. Can you suggest reasons why the CIA was involved in Afghanistan?*

2. *What can you learn from Source A about the intentions of the USSR towards Afghanistan?*

The attempts at *détente* in the 1970s had been quite earnest, but there were always flashpoints in the world where the Superpowers were at loggerheads. The invasion of Afghanistan was the last straw for the USA, and President Carter viewed Soviet actions as an extremely serious threat to peace. The USA saw that a Soviet-occupied Afghanistan would threaten India and Pakistan and would be a stepping-stone to possible Soviet control of much of the West's oil supplies. During the five years after the Soviet invasion, relations between the two Superpowers deteriorated considerably. The newly elected US president, Ronald Reagan, was keen to challenge the USSR and re-establish the USA as the leading Superpower. This chapter looks at Reagan's policies and the USSR's eventual acceptance that there had to be radical changes in its relations with the USA.

This chapter answers the following questions:

- How did Reagan change US foreign policy?
- Why did Reagan develop the Star Wars programme?
- How did relations develop from 1980–85?

Exam skills

This chapter gives guidance on how to answer Question 6 on Paper 1. This question is worth 13 marks and asks you to explain the causes of an important change. You will also be assessed for the accuracy of your spelling, punctuation and grammar, which is worth an additional 3 marks.

How did Reagan change US foreign policy?

Ronald Reagan defeated Carter in the 1980 presidential election. Reagan believed in taking a far tougher line with the Soviet Union than Carter.

President Reagan at a press conference in the early 1980s

Reagan and the 'Second Cold War'

Fighting communism became the major emphasis of Reagan's policy and he made it clear that he intended to confront the Soviet Union whenever possible. This change of policy has been called the 'Second Cold War'. Reagan was aware of the arsenal that the Soviet Union had built-up but he was determined not to be intimidated by it.

Reagan placed less emphasis on human rights and was keen to increase US defence spending. He wanted to raise the USA to the position it had held in world affairs after the Second World War. Moreover, he wanted to eradicate the humiliation of the loss of the Vietnam War, the hostage crisis in Iran and loss of prestige to the Soviet Union in Africa and Central America.

Task

1. *Use Sources A and B and your own knowledge to explain President Reagan's attitude towards communism and the Soviet Union.*

Reagan's defence policy

Reagan announced that the US defence programme between 1981–87 would cost more than a trillion dollars. The defence programme included:

- 100 MX missiles.
- 100 B-1 long-range and supersonic bombers.
- The construction of a new Stealth bomber that would be invisible to radar.
- The construction of six Trident nuclear submarines.
- The strengthening of the military communications systems.
- The development of the neutron bomb (this weapon killed people but did little damage to property).

As a result of the deployment of Soviet SS20 missiles in the western Soviet Union, the USA decided to place Cruise Missiles (these could not be detected by radar) in western Europe.

The result was a worsening of Superpower relations.

There was a view that Reagan and his advisers felt that they could win a limited nuclear war (**Nuclear Utilization Target Selection – NUTS**) against the Soviet Union. Tension began to rise because up to this point, both Superpowers had accepted the **MAD** theory.

Reagan was prepared to discuss arms limitation, but he knew he was approaching talks from a position of strength because of the economic problems that the Soviet Union was experiencing. In November 1981 President Reagan proposed his controversial 'zero option' – to cancel deployment of new US intermediate-range missiles in western Europe in return for Soviet dismantling of comparable forces (600 SS20 missiles). Brezhnev rejected the offer. Some historians think that Reagan knew Brezhnev would refuse the 'zero option' and this would mean that the USA could then place even greater numbers of missiles in Europe.

In a speech to the British House of Commons on the 8 June 1982, Reagan called the Soviet Union 'an evil empire'. Later in the year, the new leader of the Soviet Union, Yuri Andropov, responded by calling the US President insane and a liar. After this, Andropov let loose a barrage of harsh verbal assaults on the USA reminiscent of the early years of the Cold War. Moscow repeatedly accused President Reagan of fanning the flames of war and compared him to Hitler.

Tasks

2. *Study Source C. Can you suggest reasons why the USA was prepared to consider the idea of NUTS?*

3. *Look at Source D. What message is the cartoonist trying to put across about relations between the USA and the Soviet Union? Can you suggest what the cartoonist's attitude towards each leader is?*

Source C: **Map showing the deployment of nuclear missiles in Europe in the early 1980s**

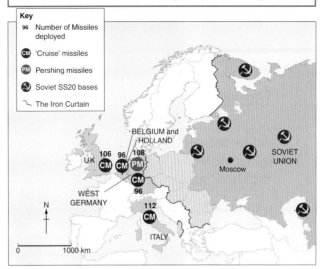

Source D: **A cartoon about President Reagan (left) published in the USA in 1982**

On 23 March 1983, President Reagan announced the Strategic Defence Initiative (SDI), quickly nicknamed 'Star Wars' by the media. SDI was a plan for a ground- and space-based, laser-armed anti-ballistic missile system that, if deployed, would create a shield for US land-based missiles.

Four days after the President's announcement, and in direct response to it, Andropov spoke out firmly. He accused the USA of preparing a first-strike attack on the Soviet Union and asserted that President Reagan was 'inventing new plans on how to unleash a nuclear war in the best way, in the hope of winning it'. Andropov saw that SDI would give the USA an advantage in any conflict and would then readily consider a tactical nuclear war. The US Congress voted in favour of funds for the development of SDI.

Andropov and his advisers realised that the 'Star Wars' programme meant that they would have to spend even more money on armaments in order to compete with the USA. The Soviet economy was already experiencing problems and renewed arms spending might destroy it completely. Part of Reagan's plan was that the Soviet Union would try to compete and, in so doing, its economy would collapse.

Task

3. Copy and complete the diagram below to illustrate SDI (Star Wars) and its impact. Complete it by answering the questions in the circles.

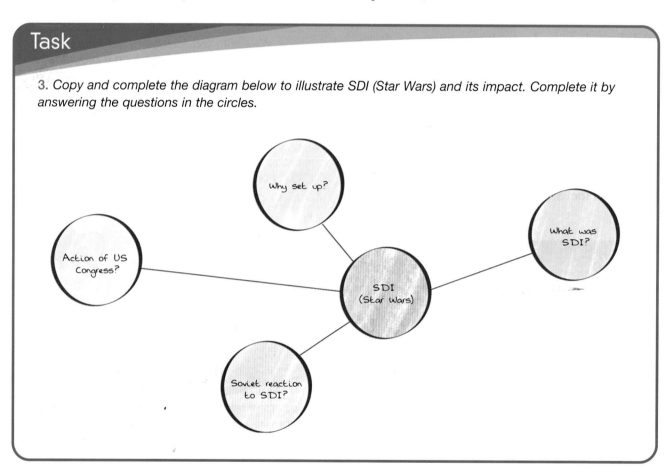

How did relations develop from 1980–85?

The changing leaders of the Soviet Union, 1982–85

Leonid Brezhnev, leader of the Soviet Union, 1964–82

Yuri Andropov, leader of the Soviet Union from November 1982 to February 1984

Brezhnev died in 1982, and the new leader, Andropov, died shortly after in February 1984. Superpowers relations fluctuated during this period, and it was difficult to establish continuity.

In 1983 Reagan permitted the sale of US grain to the Soviet Union in what turned out to be the biggest ever trade agreement between the two countries. It is quite paradoxical that Reagan had to rely on the Soviet Union to help the US economy. Nevertheless, relations were still sour, and Chernenko, who succeeded Andropov as General Secretary, was quick to announce the Soviet boycott of the US Olympic Games in Los Angeles in 1984.

Chernenko accused the United States of manipulating the games for political purposes and using propaganda against the Soviet Union. He also claimed that security precautions for Soviet athletes were inadequate. A spokesperson for President Reagan said the Soviet Union needed to consider its 'barbarous' actions in Afghanistan and its treatment of dissidents, such as Andrei Sakharov.

The USA saw the boycott as a simple retaliation for the events of 1980 at the Moscow games. The Soviet decision was supported by its allies in the Warsaw Pact (except Romania and Yugoslavia), Afghanistan, Angola, Cuba, Ethiopia, Laos, Mongolia, North Korea and Vietnam. However, the USA could claim that the games were the biggest ever because a record 140 nations participated, including China (for the first time since 1932).

Just as in 1980, the boycotting nations held their own alternative games, known as the Friendship Games. The boycott again seemed to show that the world was divided into two camps, even in sport.

There was a hint that the Superpowers were more willing to resume the search for *détente* towards the end of 1984. There was a great fear in Europe that the installation of Cruise and Pershing missiles had brought the possibility of a tactical nuclear war closer (NUTS – see page 89). There had been many anti-nuclear demonstrations in the countries where Cruise and Pershing missiles were stationed. There were even demonstrations within the USA.

The turning point occurred after the death of Chernenko and with the appointment of Mikhail Gorbachev as the new Soviet leader in March 1985. Gorbachev was much younger than his predecessors and he was prepared to adopt drastic policies to improve Superpower relations. He had to attempt to improve the relationship, as he knew that, without change, the Soviet Union would collapse. The changes brought in by Gorbachev are discussed in the next chapter.

Konstantin Chernenko, leader of the Soviet Union, February 1984 to March 1985

Source A: A Soviet poster entitled 'America' (1983)

Mikhail Gorbachev, leader of the Soviet Union, 1985–91

Tasks

1. *What can you learn from Source A about the Soviet attitude to the USA in 1983?*

2. *Working in groups, divide into Pessimists and Optimists. The Pessimists should prepare a case which argues that nuclear war was a distinct probability by 1985. The Optimists should prepare a case arguing that the danger of nuclear war was not so great by 1985. Each should present their case and a vote should be taken on the more convincing.*

Examination practice

This section provides guidance on how to answer Question 6 from Paper 1, which is worth 13 marks and asks you to give an extended explanation of several reasons for change. You will also be given up to 3 marks for the quality of your spelling, punctuation and grammar so there are 16 marks in total for Question 6.

Question 6 – 13-mark essay question

Explain why relations between the USA and the Soviet Union changed in the years 1980–85.
You may use the following in your answer:
- The Soviet invasion of Afghanistan
- The election of Ronald Reagan as President of the USA

You must also include information of your own.

How to answer

- Look for the key points in the question and underline them. In this case it's: Explain why **relations between the USA and the Soviet Union** changed in the years **1980–85**.
- Give at least three reasons, and support each with detail, showing how it caused a change in relations between the USA and the Soviet Union. Three is important because you must bring in a reason of your own, as well as more detail about the two provided in the question.

- Use linking words between each reason and the next (see examples on page 96).
  Say something about the importance of each reason and, in your conclusion, say which you think is the most important.

The diagram on page 96 shows you the steps you should take to write a good answer to this kind of question. Use the steps and examples to complete the answer to the question by writing each paragraph and linking them where possible. Alternatively you could use the grid below to structure your answer to the question.

When they mark your answer to this question, examiners will also award up to 3 marks for the quality of your **spelling**, **punctuation** and **grammar**. To get full marks you need to be accurate in all three of these. The best way to prepare for this is to start taking care over your spelling, punctuation and grammar in the months before your exam, raising your own standards. (These extra marks for spelling, punctuation and grammar apply in many subjects, so it's worth getting better at them).

It also helps you to get all the extra marks if you use special historical words and phrases. In this question, some examples would be: *détente*, arms race, Superpower, communist and anti-communist.

INTRODUCTION
Set the scene for your essay by explaining the question and listing the main reasons your answer will include.

FIRST PARAGRAPH – FIRST REASON FOR CHANGE
- Introduce the first reason for change and then fully explain it.
- Make a judgement about the importance of this reason. Do the same for each reason that you explain.

Link to second reason

SECOND PARAGRAPH – SECOND REASON FOR CHANGE

Link to third reason

THIRD PARAGRAPH – THIRD REASON FOR CHANGE

CONCLUSION
Explain which you think was the most important (fundamental) reason and why.

Examination practice

STEP 1
Write an introduction that identifies the key issues you need to cover in your answer and your main argument.

Example:
Relations changed between the USA and the Soviet Union in the years 1980-85 because détente was destroyed following the Soviet invasion of Afghanistan which then led to a renewed arms race.

STEP 2
After your introduction, write a good length paragraph on the reason for change. The first sentence of this paragraph has been done for you. Complete it by explaining that the invasion damaged SALT II and led to the Moscow Olympics boycott; then explain how this caused a deterioration of relations.

Example:
The Soviet invasion of Afghanistan worsened relations with the USA because it undid the good work of the 1970s...

STEP 3
Make a judgement on the importance of this reason. In other words, prioritise it. Was it the most important, quite important or of little importance?

Example:
The invasion was one of the most important reasons because it meant that trust between the Superpowers was broken and it led to the USA becoming more prepared to challenge the Soviet Union.

STEP 4
Try to make links between each of the reasons (paragraphs). Remember the link words or phrases mentioned on the previous page. This is an example of a possible link between the first reason and the second reason (the election of Ronald Reagan).

Example:
Furthermore, this led to the election of Ronald Reagan, who was fiercely anti-communist.

STEP 5
Now the link has been made, go back to step 2 and repeat the steps until you have covered all the reasons. You should aim to give at least three reasons.

Have a go yourself

STEP 6
Write a conclusion making your final judgement on the question. In other words, what do you think to have been the most important reason(s)? Explain why. You could begin this final paragraph with the word 'overall'.

Example:
Overall, the most important reason for the change in relations in the years 1980-85 was the work of President Reagan. He was determined to overcome the Soviet threat. However, the leaders of the Soviet Union were so unwilling to yield that their role is significant. A worsening of the situation was the result. It was only when Gorbachev, a much younger leader, emerged that relations began to improve again.

10 Gorbachev and the end of the Cold War

Source A: **Photograph of General Secretary Gorbachev and President Bush meeting in Malta, December 1989. At this meeting, they declared that the Cold War was over**

Tasks

1. *What can you learn from Source A about the relationship between the two Superpower leaders?*

Détente had failed and, by 1985, many people were convinced that a limited nuclear war was now on the agenda of the Superpowers. They saw the development of the Strategic Defence Initiative (see pages 91–92) and the deployment of large numbers of missiles in Europe as evidence of this. The increase in the US defence budget, problems in Africa, the Middle East and the Afghanistan War showed that the Cold War was just as dangerous to world peace as it had ever been.

Yet, by 1989, Bush and Gorbachev were able to announce that the Cold War was over. This was a remarkable turnaround in just four years.

This chapter answers the following questions:

• What was Gorbachev's role in ending the Cold War?
• How did the arms race end?
• Why did the Soviet Union collapse so quickly?

Exam skills

At the end of this chapter are further examples of some of the highest scoring question on Paper 1, Question 5. These questions are designed to test your knowledge of the whole period covered by this book.

What was Gorbachev's role in ending the Cold War?

The Cold War came to an end when Gorbachev decided to call it off unilaterally, a move that caught the USA and the West off guard. His immediate abandonment of the Brezhnev Doctrine (see page 56) was a clear sign of his 'new thinking'. He did this because the Cold War was draining so much of the Soviet Union's wealth that it could not continue to develop economically, and the falling standard of living was creating unrest in the country. Gorbachev also took this step because he wanted to reform the Communist Party in the Soviet Union and modernise Soviet-style socialism. He did not intend to abandon it.

There were three important strategies through which he ended the Cold War:

- He initiated sweeping reforms in the Communist Party and Soviet system in the Soviet Union – *perestroika* (restructuring) and *glasnost* (openness).
- He ended the arms race with the USA and signed various arms reduction agreements.
- He stopped Soviet interference in eastern European satellite states like Poland, Czechoslovakia and other Warsaw Pact countries.

Gorbachev wanted to maintain the Soviet Union's role of Superpower. He knew that he had to win over the Soviet people and show the world that he would not threaten world peace. He had to be all things to all people.

Gorbachev had been in power only a month when he roamed around an industrial district of Moscow, visiting supermarkets, chatting with workers at a truck factory (see Source C), discussing computer training with teachers at a school and nurses' pay with the staff at a hospital.

Tasks

1. *What can you learn from Source A about Gorbachev as leader of the Soviet Union?*

2. *Read Source B. What can you learn about the problems facing Gorbachev in 1985?*

3. *Describe one reason why Gorbachev ended the Cold War.*

4. *Working in pairs, copy and complete the table below.*

Why were Gorbachev's changes necessary?	Can you suggest any dangers that Gorbachev might have faced when introducing such major changes?

He even dropped into a young couple's apartment for tea. That was the first of the walkabouts that took him all over the Soviet Union, from Murmansk in the North to Kamchatka on the shores of the Pacific. When he visited the Baltic Shipyards in Leningrad, a spokesman for the workers began a monotone welcoming speech expressing a wish that *perestroika* would develop even faster. Gorbachev interrupted with playful cries of '*Davai! Davai!*' (Let's go to it!), drawing a big laugh from the crowd.

Dissidents were released from jail, banned books were published and the Soviet people learned of the atrocities committed when Stalin was in power. However, *glasnost* was a two-edged sword for Gorbachev. The more freedom people gained, the more they wanted and the more they began to criticise Gorbachev – making it more difficult to maintain the Communist Party in power.

The economy had been damaged by the arms race, the space race, the war in Afghanistan and

Source C: Photograph of Gorbachev visiting a truck factory in April 1985. This visit was seen as the beginning of his restructuring and economic acceleration programme

above all by a system that did not encourage incentive. *Perestroika* (restructuring), and *uskorenie* ('acceleration' of economic development) did bring some considerable changes, and certain aspects of a free economy were introduced. Reforms in the political system, such as elections for local government, did win support for Gorbachev and enabled him to be equally radical in his dealings with the USA.

Source D: From an article in the *Sunday Times*, 27 December 1987. The article was discussing Gorbachev's impact on the Soviet Union and the world

The Soviet Union is different thanks to Gorbachev. In the world beyond the Soviet Union he has been the prime instigator of change. At home the changes are most remarkable. Compared with just one year ago, Soviet citizens can now think more freely almost without fear of reprisal. They can emigrate in increasing – though still small – numbers. Seeing and reading certain plays, films and novels which were once banned is now no longer considered dangerous. Nevertheless, some foreign radio stations are still jammed and there are still political prisoners.

Tasks

4. Write a speech, as if by Gorbachev, explaining how your work in the Soviet Union is linked to the change in relations with the USA.

5. Look at Source D. What can you learn about the extent of the changes Gorbachev was introducing?

6. Briefly explain the key features of Gorbachev's reforms in the Soviet Union.

How did the arms race end?

Arms limitation talks were renewed after it was clear that Gorbachev was keen to change relations with the West. A summit meeting between Gorbachev and Reagan was held in Geneva over two days in November 1985. At the meeting Reagan would not give up his commitment to the 'Star Wars' defence system (SDI) but at the end of discussions both Reagan and Gorbachev spoke of the world being a 'safer place'.

The two leaders broke with convention and met together without advisers to discuss issues on their own. Though nothing concrete was decided, the Geneva Accord was set out. This committed the two countries to:

• speed up arms talks
• work towards the abolition of chemical weapons
• be more active on issues of human rights.

Both leaders promised to meet again in the near future. It was clear to many observers that the two men had been able to be amicable despite the poor relations between their two countries in the early 1980s. A second meeting was eventually set for October 1986 in Iceland.

Source B: **Photograph of President Reagan (centre) and General Secretary Gorbachev (left) signing the INF Treaty at the White House on 8 December 1987**

The 1986 summit meeting in Reykjavik

The summit meeting between President Reagan and Soviet leader Mikhail Gorbachev collapsed after the two leaders had tentatively agreed to sweeping reductions in nuclear arsenals but became deadlocked again on the crucial issue of restricting the US space-based missile defence programme – Star Wars (SDI). Gorbachev, in a news conference, painted a bleak picture of US–Soviet relations leading up to the summit and said that the talks had broken down over the fundamental differences between the Superpowers on the Strategic Defence Initiative and the Anti-Ballistic Missile treaty. He said Reagan's insistence on deploying SDI had 'frustrated and scuttled' the opportunity for an agreement.

The Intermediate Nuclear Forces Treaty (INF) of 1987

A third summit was held in December 1987, and a breakthrough was achieved with the agreement of the Intermediate Nuclear Forces Treaty (INF). The treaty eliminated nuclear and **conventional** ground-launched ballistic and cruise missiles with ranges of 500 to 5500 kilometers (300 to 3400 miles). By the treaty's deadline, 1 June 1991, a total of 2692 of such weapons had been destroyed, 846 by the USA and 1846 by the Soviet Union. Also under the treaty, both nations were allowed to inspect each other's military installations.

Under the INF, there were to be stringent verification procedures to check that nuclear weapons were destroyed. Reagan described INF as the realisation of 'an impossible vision' and Gorbachev stated it had 'universal significance for mankind'. Both leaders stressed that INF was only the first step towards an even more radical agreement to half long-range nuclear weapons. Hopefully, this treaty would be signed in Moscow in 1988.

Gorbymania

After the INF Treaty, the final summit meeting was held in Moscow in May 1988. By this time, much of the West seemed to be overtaken by what became known as 'Gorbymania'. It was as if Gorbachev had become a pop star. Furthermore, it was evident that the wives of Reagan and Gorbachev had played a role in pushing the two leaders together. Crowds were happy to watch them wherever they went. This was all very different from the dark days of the Cold War of the 1950s and early 1980s.

> **Source C:** Photograph of Nancy Reagan (right) and Raisa Gorbacheva (left) at the INF Summit

Tasks

1. Working in pairs, explain exactly what Gorbachev meant in Source A.

2. Why did some people think that his message in Source A was revolutionary for a Soviet leader?

3. Why were initial talks between Reagan and Gorbachev unsuccessful?

4. Conduct your own research into 'Gorbymania' and the roles of Nancy Reagan and Raisa Gorbacheva. Write up what you discover.

Source D: US experts verifying the destruction of nuclear weapons in the Soviet Union in 1988 after the INF Treaty

Source E: Gorbachev and George Bush Senior at the Malta Summit, 1989

The Conventional Armed Forces in Europe (CFE) treaty

At the Moscow summit, there were more arms control talks and there were troop reductions in Europe in 1989. Moreover, Gorbachev's promise to withdraw troops from Afghanistan showed his peaceful intentions. The summit led to the Conventional Armed Forces in Europe Treaty (CFE) which was signed by NATO and Warsaw Pact representatives in November 1990. The agreement reduced the number of tanks, missiles, aircraft and other forms of non-nuclear military hardware held by signatory states. The USA and the Soviet Union continued to enjoy good relations. The new US president George Bush Senior and Gorbachev were able to announce that the Cold War was over in a summit in Malta in 1989.

When Saddam Hussein invaded Kuwait in 1990, the two Superpowers acted closely and followed the directives of the **United Nations**. However, Gorbachev did not commit any Soviet troops to the Coalition Forces that invaded Iraq.

START talks, 1990–91

At the Washington summit of 31 May–3 June 1990, Bush and Gorbachev discussed Strategic Arms Limitations (START) and finally signed the Treaty for the Reduction and Limitation of Strategic Offensive Arms (START I), on 31 July 1991. It called for both sides to reduce their strategic nuclear forces over seven years to:

- 1600 strategic nuclear delivery vehicles (SNDVs) and 6000 warheads
- a limit of 4900 on ballistic missiles.

This meant reducing 25 to 35 per cent of all their strategic warheads. Bush and Gorbachev signed the treaty with pens made from scrapped missiles.

Tasks

5. *Briefly explain the key features of relations between the USA and the Soviet Union in the years 1984–87.*

6. *Look at Source D. What can you learn about the INF Treaty from this source?*

Why did the Soviet Union collapse so quickly?

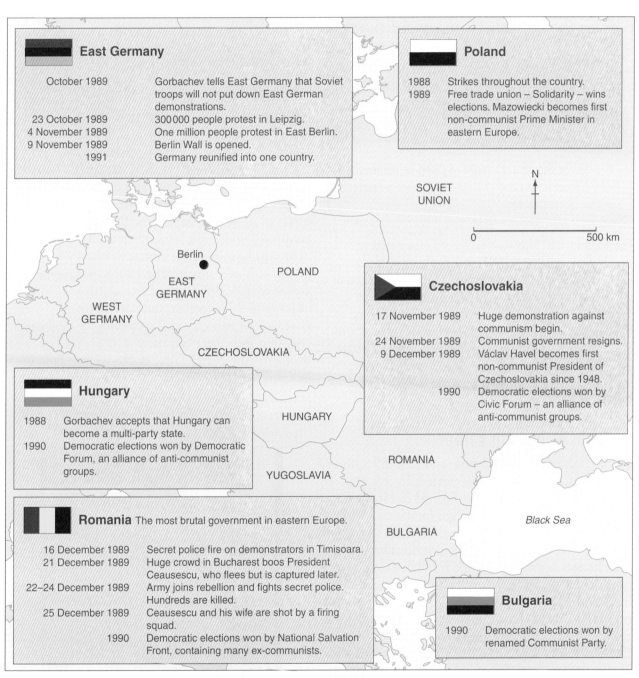

East Germany

October 1989	Gorbachev tells East Germany that Soviet troops will not put down East German demonstrations.
23 October 1989	300000 people protest in Leipzig.
4 November 1989	One million people protest in East Berlin.
9 November 1989	Berlin Wall is opened.
1991	Germany reunified into one country.

Poland

1988	Strikes throughout the country.
1989	Free trade union – Solidarity – wins elections. Mazowiecki becomes first non-communist Prime Minister in eastern Europe.

SOVIET UNION

N

0   500 km

Berlin

POLAND

EAST GERMANY

WEST GERMANY

Czechoslovakia

17 November 1989	Huge demonstration against communism begin.
24 November 1989	Communist government resigns.
9 December 1989	Václav Havel becomes first non-communist President of Czechoslovakia since 1948.
1990	Democratic elections won by Civic Forum – an alliance of anti-communist groups.

CZECHOSLOVAKIA

Hungary

1988	Gorbachev accepts that Hungary can become a multi-party state.
1990	Democratic elections won by Democratic Forum, an alliance of anti-communist groups.

HUNGARY

ROMANIA

YUGOSLAVIA

Romania The most brutal government in eastern Europe.

16 December 1989	Secret police fire on demonstrators in Timisoara.
21 December 1989	Huge crowd in Bucharest boos President Ceausescu, who flees but is captured later.
22–24 December 1989	Army joins rebellion and fights secret police. Hundreds are killed.
25 December 1989	Ceausescu and his wife are shot by a firing squad.
1990	Democratic elections won by National Salvation Front, containing many ex-communists.

Black Sea

BULGARIA

Bulgaria

1990	Democratic elections won by renamed Communist Party.

Map showing the break-up of the Soviet Empire in the years 1988–91

Task

1. Look at Source A. Work in pairs to discuss why this is a surprising comment from a leader of the Soviet Union.

Gorbachev had shown that he was prepared to make deals with the USA and to think the unthinkable. The Soviet economy could no longer stand the strain of supporting forces in eastern Europe. He went even further when he rejected the Brezhnev Doctrine in 1988 (see page 82), and in 1989 he accepted that members of the Warsaw Pact could make changes to their own countries without expecting outside interference. This became known as the Sinatra Doctrine.

Changes in eastern Europe

Reform started in Poland first, and in 1989 a non-communist government was elected. In that year, a range of political parties was formed in Hungary and free elections were proposed for 1990. Gorbachev did not interfere and began to withdraw Soviet troops from Hungary. The key to the changes in eastern Europe in 1989 was Hungary's decision to open its border with Austria in May of that year. This meant that there was now a hole in the Iron Curtain (see page 19). This created a way for East Germans to move to West Germany. It brought into question whether the Berlin Wall and the Iron Curtain could continue to exist.

Events in East and West Germany

Demonstrations occurred in East Germany in 1989 and there were calls for changes to the system of government. Gorbachev visited East Germany in October 1989 and informed political leaders that the Soviet Union would not become involved in its internal affairs. Demonstrations continued and, on 4 November, the largest demonstration in East Germany's history took place, with over one million people in East Berlin demanding democracy and free elections. On the evening of 9 November, the East German government announced the opening of the border crossings into West Germany. The people began to dismantle the Berlin Wall. Within a few days, over one million people per day had seized the chance

Source C: The cover of *Time* magazine on 20 November 1989

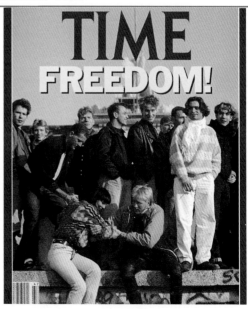

Source D: Photograph of demonstrators breaking down the Berlin Wall, November 1989

to see relatives and experience life in the West. West and East Germany were formally reunited on 3 October 1990.

Tension in the world seemed to ease by the day while the power of the Soviet Union seemed to be dwindling so quickly. The new Germany joined NATO and, in 1991, the Warsaw Pact was dissolved.

The collapse of the Soviet Union

Events in eastern Europe had a catastrophic impact on the Soviet Union. The many nationalities and ethnic groups saw how the satellite states had been able to break away from Moscow.

In 1990, the Baltic states of Estonia, Latvia and Lithuania declared themselves independent, which was accepted by Moscow in 1991. This led to other demands for independence within the Soviet Union. There were fears that the country was about to disintegrate, and Gorbachev found that he was opposed by most sections of Soviet society.

There was an attempted *coup d'état* in August 1991, which was defeated by Boris Yeltsin (President of the Russian Socialist Republic) and though Gorbachev was restored, he had lost authority. Gorbachev resigned in December 1991 and the Soviet Union split into several independent states (see map).

Tasks

2. *Describe one reason why the Berlin Wall was dismantled.*

3. *What can you learn about the breaking down of the Berlin Wall from Sources C and D?*

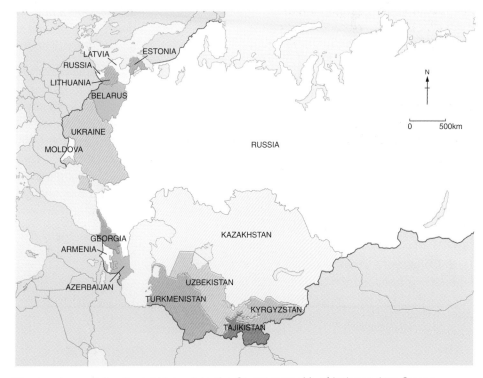

The break-up of the Soviet Union into the Commonwealth of Independent States

The Cold War had officially ended in 1989, and now there was only one Superpower left – the USA.

Assessment of Gorbachev

By 1990, Gorbachev's actions had won him the **Nobel Peace Prize**. It is doubtful this would have been awarded without a consideration of his approach to the satellite states of eastern Europe. His policies had reduced the fears of the USA. Gorbachev and Reagan had become personal friends and had therefore made some significant agreements. These agreements meant that the USA no longer regarded the Soviet Union as a major threat. The INF Treaty was especially important, although the removal of Soviet troops from Afghanistan, not interfering in the anti-communist revolutions in eastern Europe and *glasnost*, all combined to end the Cold War.

> **Source E:** An extract from the citation of the Nobel Peace Prize Committee, 1990
>
> *The Nobel Committee has decided to award the 1990 Peace Prize to Mikhail Gorbachev, President of the Soviet Union, for his leading role in the peace process. During the last few years, dramatic changes have taken place in the relationship between East and West. Confrontation has been replaced by negotiations. Old European nations have been allowed to regain their freedom. The arms race is slowing down and we see a definite and active process in the direction of arms control and disarmament. These historic changes spring from several factors, but in 1990 the Nobel Committee wants to honour Mikhail Gorbachev. The greater openness he has brought about in Soviet society has also helped promote international trust.*

Tasks

4. *Construct a flow chart to show how the Soviet Empire fell apart (begin and end as follows):*

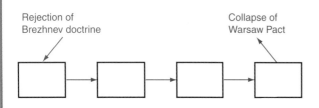

5. *Briefly explain the key features of the collapse of the Soviet Empire.*

6. *Describe one reason why Gorbachev won the Nobel Prize in 1990.*

7. *What can you learn from Source E about Gorbachev's role in ending the Cold War?*

8. *Construct a timeline showing developments in relations between the Superpowers from*

1985–90. *Place positive developments above the line and negative ones below. Explain why each was positive/negative.*

9. *In groups, write an obituary for the Cold War, as if it were a human being. Cover its birth, death, high points, low points, positive outcomes and offer an overall judgement.*

10. *Interview some of your parents, relatives or teachers to gather first-hand accounts about the Cold War – the key events of this topic may have happened in their lifetimes. Ask them about their attitudes to the USA and the Soviet Union, where they were when certain crises occurred, what it was like living under the threat of a nuclear war, if their life was changed by any event in the Cold War, etc.*

11. *Explain why the events of 1985–90 helped to end Cold War by 1990.*

Examination practice

This section provides some more examples of questions in the style of the highest-scoring question on Paper 1, Question 5.

The purpose of Question 5 is to make sure you know about the whole Unit, not just bits of it, so the four bullet points are drawn from across the whole course. Look back to page 73 to see what these questions are like and an example of how to write a good answer.

To get full marks you have to:

• Choose three out of the four items you are given which you know plenty about. (This really turns Question 5 into three shorter questions).

• Make sure you show how the event you are writing about links to the big theme in the question

• Make sure you show the importance of the event you are writing about to the big theme.

Notice that some events appear in more than one example e.g. the Cuban Missile crisis, 1962. However, your answer will be different in each case because you will have to show its importance to different big themes.

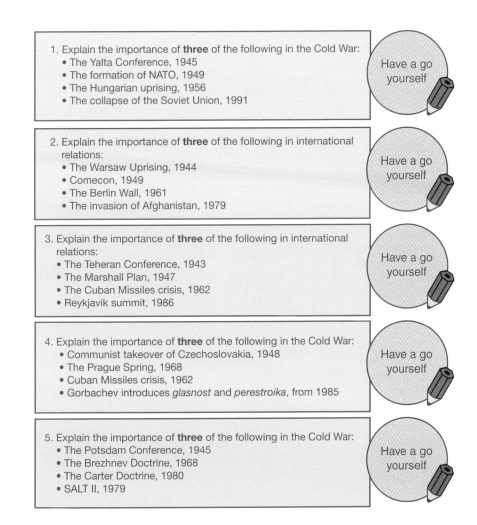

1. Explain the importance of **three** of the following in the Cold War:
   • The Yalta Conference, 1945
   • The formation of NATO, 1949
   • The Hungarian uprising, 1956
   • The collapse of the Soviet Union, 1991

Have a go yourself

2. Explain the importance of **three** of the following in international relations:
   • The Warsaw Uprising, 1944
   • Comecon, 1949
   • The Berlin Wall, 1961
   • The invasion of Afghanistan, 1979

Have a go yourself

3. Explain the importance of **three** of the following in international relations:
   • The Teheran Conference, 1943
   • The Marshall Plan, 1947
   • The Cuban Missiles crisis, 1962
   • Reykjavik summit, 1986

Have a go yourself

4. Explain the importance of **three** of the following in the Cold War:
   • Communist takeover of Czechoslovakia, 1948
   • The Prague Spring, 1968
   • Cuban Missiles crisis, 1962
   • Gorbachev introduces *glasnost* and *perestroika*, from 1985

Have a go yourself

5. Explain the importance of **three** of the following in the Cold War:
   • The Potsdam Conference, 1945
   • The Brezhnev Doctrine, 1968
   • The Carter Doctrine, 1980
   • SALT II, 1979

Have a go yourself

Revision activities

Part 1: How did the Cold War develop? 1943–56

1. Are the following statements about the origins of the Cold War true or false?

    (a) The two Superpowers after 1945 were Britain and the Soviet Union.

    (b) Churchill, Truman and Attlee attended the Potsdam Conference.

    (c) The Western Powers supported the Bolsheviks during the Russian Civil War.

    (d) The Nazi-Soviet Pact was signed in 1941.

    (e) Roosevelt, Churchill and Stalin attended the Yalta Conference.

2. Put the following events in chronological order:

    • Potsdam Conference • Teheran Conference • Yalta Conference • Formation of the Grand Alliance

3. This account of the Truman Doctrine and the Marshall Plan is by a student who has not revised thoroughly. Re-write it, correcting the errors.

    > In 1945, Truman, the prime minister of the USA, announced support for the government of Greece which was being threatened by fascists. This was a policy of containment and was known as the Churchill Doctrine. Truman also decided to give economic aid to countries in Europe recovering after the war. This was known as the Truman Doctrine. Stalin was delighted with this aid and encouraged countries in Eastern Europe to accept assistance from the USA.

4. Below is a list of events that affected relations between East and West in the years 1945–47. Place them in order of importance, from most important to least important. Give a brief explanation for your decision.

    • Soviet expansion into Eastern Europe
    • Iron Curtain speech
    • Truman Doctrine
    • Marshall Plan

5. Decide whether each of the following items is a cause, event or consequence of the Berlin Crisis of 1948–9.

    • Stalin turned the eastern zone into the German Democratic Republic.
    • British and US planes made 193,350 flights during the airlift.
    • The Allies set up their own currency in the Western zone.
    • During the airlift West Berliners were supplied with 4000 tons per day.
    • It led to the setting up of NATO.
    • The West zone recovered quickly because of Marshall Aid.

6. The numbers game. How many...

    • Allied zones in Germany? • Countries in NATO when it was first set up? • Countries in the Warsaw Pact when it was set up?

7. Match the following causes and effects of the Hungarian Crisis of 1956:

Causes
2. Nagy was determined to introduce reforms.
3. Khrushchev was anxious not to appear weak to other members of the Warsaw Pact.
4. Western countries did not intervene to help the Hungarian rebels.
Effects
a. He introduced free elections and ended the one-party system.
b. On 4 November 1956 Soviet troops and tanks invaded Hungary.
c. They were preoccupied with the Suez Crisis.
d. He killed 2000 in purges and imprisoned a further 200,000.

8. What explanation can you give for the following contradictory statements?

    • The West opposed the Soviet invasion of Hungary and yet did nothing.
    • Khrushchev carried out a policy of de-Stalinisation and yet invaded Hungary in 1956.

Part 2: Three Cold War crises: Berlin, Cuba and Czechoslovakia, 1957–69

1. Explain in no more than one sentence what you know about the following:
   - The U-2 spy plane, 1960 • East German refugees and West Berlin • Vienna Summit, 1961 • 'Ich bin ein Berliner'

2. Write a paragraph explaining why you agree or disagree with each of the following statements:
   (a) The building of the Berlin Wall was a victory for the Soviet Union in the Cold War.
   b) The building of the Berlin Wall showed that Kennedy was a weak leader.

3. Construct a mind map showing the following main reasons for the Cuban Missiles Crisis:
   - Castro in power • Trade issues with the USA
   - Bay of Pigs • Arms race • Soviet trade with Cuba • Castro's political views • US missiles in Europe

   On your mind map:
   - Draw a line showing links between at least two of the reasons. On the line briefly explain the link.
   - Indicate which you think was the most important reason. Give a brief explanation for your choice.

4. What explanation can you give for the following statements?

- Kennedy was successful in the Cuban Missiles crisis because the Soviet Union dismantled the sites.
- Khrushchev was successful in the Cuban Missiles crisis because the USA dismantled missile sites in Turkey.

5. Construct a mind map showing the following main reasons for the Soviet invasion of Czechoslovakia in 1968:
   - Czech economy • Soviet control • Events of 1948 • Reforms of Dubcek • Attitude of Brezhnev • Attitude of Warsaw Pact countries

   On your mind map:
   - Draw a line showing links between at least two of the reasons. On the line briefly explain the link.
   - Indicate which you think was the most important reason. Give a brief explanation for your choice.

6. Write a paragraph explaining why you agree or disagree with each of the following statements:
   (a) The most important consequence of the Soviet invasion of Czechoslovakia was the Brezhnev Doctrine.
   b) The Soviet Union had no choice but to invade Czechoslovakia in 1968.

Part 3: Why did the Cold War end? 1979–91

1. Below is a list of events that affected relations between East and West in the 1970s. Place them in order of importance, from most important to least important. Give a brief explanation for your decision.
   - *Détente*
   - SALT 1
   - Helsinki Agreements
   - Invasion of Afghanistan

2. 'In the years to 1979, after SALT I, *détente* failed.' Write two paragraphs disagreeing with this statement.

3. Explain in no more than one sentence what you know about the following:
   - 'Evil empire' • SDI • Cruise missiles • NUTS • MAD

4. Put the following events in chronological order:
   - Gorbachev became leader of the Soviet Union
   - SDI programme announced • Moscow Olympic Games boycotted • Death of Andropov • Death of Brezhnev • Los Angeles Olympic Games boycotted

5. Summarise in no more than ten words the importance of the following in the Cold War in the 1980s and 1990s:
   - Soviet economic problems • The effects of the Afghan War on the Soviet Union • START • Sinatra Doctrine

6. 'Gorbachev was more important than Reagan in ending the Cold War.'
   Do you agree? Make a list of ways in which Gorbachev was more important and a list of ways in which Reagan was more important. Give brief explanations in each case.

Glossary

ABM An Anti-Ballistic Missile is one designed to counter inter-continental ballistic missiles, the strategic ballistic missiles used to deliver nuclear weapons or their elements in flight. ABMs may also be used against chemical or biological payloads.

Allied Control Commission The body set up by the Allies to run Hungary until a suitable government was elected.

Berlin Ultimatum Khrushchev's 1958 threat to the western Allies to leave Berlin in 6 months and turn it into a neutral free city.

Bizonia As part of the Allied decision to allow some economic revival in Germany, the US and British zones were merged in January 1948 into one unit, called Bizonia.

Bolshevik Member of the Russian Bolshevik Party that seized power in 1917 and set up a communist state.

Brezhnev Doctrine Soviet foreign policy which called for military intervention by Warsaw Pact forces if another member of the Warsaw Pact tried to leave the Soviet sphere of influence or moderate socialism.

Brinkmanship The art of moving to the very edge of war but not engaging in it.

Carter Doctrine President Carter announced in January 1980 that the USA was prepared to use military force to protect its oil interests in the Persian Gulf region.

CIA (Central Intelligence Agency) The US office which co-ordinates and conducts espionage and intelligence activities.

Civil war A conflict fought between two sides within the same country.

Coalition government Government formed of two or more different political parties.

Collectivisation of agriculture The grouping of farms into one body that is then managed by the state.

Comecon The association of Soviet oriented communist countries set up in 1949 to co-ordinate economic development.

Cominform The Communist Information Bureau established in 1947 to exchange information among nine eastern European countries and co-ordinate their activities.

Communism A system which puts forward a classless society where private ownership has been abolished and the means of production and subsistence belong to the community.

Congress The US parliament consisting of the Senate and House of Representatives.

Containment Using US influence and military resources to prevent the expansion of communism into non-communist countries.

Conventional weapons Non-nuclear weapons.

Coup d'état An armed rebellion or revolt against the existing government.

Demilitarisation Removing all armed forces from an area.

Deployment The distribution of military forces within a given area.

De-Stalinisation The elimination of the influence of Stalin.

Détente An attempt to reduce the tension between the USA and the Soviet Union.

Dissident A person who disagrees with the government. In the Soviet Union, dissidents were often placed in work camps or placed under house arrest.

Draft system The US name for conscription. It was compulsory for men who reached the age of eighteen to serve in the armed forces.

Glasnost The name given to Gorbachev's policy of openness encouraging free expression and an end to censorship.

GNP (Gross National Product) The total value of all goods and services produced by a nation each year.

Guerrilla war Fighting in small groups against conventional forces, using such methods as sabotage, sudden ambush, etc.

Inauguration speech The formal acceptance speech of the US president on taking office.

Inter-Continental Ballistic Missiles (ICBMs) A missile that has the range to carry a nuclear bomb between continents.

Islamic fundamentalism Opposes secular western society and seeks to set up a state based on Islamic law.

MAD ('Mutually Assured Destruction') The belief that nuclear weapons made each side more secure and less likely to attack. The enemy would not dare to attack first, because if it did, the other would strike back before its bombs had landed and it too would be destroyed.

Marshall Aid The US programme of financial and economic aid given to Europe after the end of the Second World War.

Marshall Plan A special system of loans from the USA to European countries implemented at the end of the Second World War which allowed for reconstruction and economic regeneration. General George Marshall was the senior US army officer who devised the plan.

MIRV(s) A multiple independently targetable re-entry vehicle – one of a collection of nuclear weapons carried on a single ICBM or a SLBM. Using MIRVs, a single launched missile can strike several targets.

Monroe Doctrine (1823) Foreign policy statement by President Monroe which decared that Europe should not involve itself in the American continent.

Nobel Peace Prize The annual prize given for outstanding contributions to peace.

Nuclear Non-proliferation Treaty The agreement that prohibited non-nuclear weapon states from acquiring nuclear weapons by manufacture or transfer of technology.

Nuclear Utilization Target Selection (NUTS) The idea that in a nuclear war specific targets could be identified and destruction limited. It gave rise to the idea that there could be a victor in a nuclear war.

Nuclear weapons Using weapons of mass destruction.

Partial Test Ban Treaty The 1963 agreement that prohibited nuclear testing in the atmosphere, outer space and underwater.

People's democracy A system of governing a country, either directly by the people or by holding regular elections to some form of parliament which makes the law.

Perestroika The name given to Gorbachev's policy for economic restructuring.

Pitched battle(s) Battle fought in open country between the armies of the two sides.

Politburo The central body of the Communist Party that makes all the important decisions.

Purge(s) The elimination of opponents from a state or political party.

Republic A country in which the head of state is an elected president.

Royalist government A government run by a monarchy, such as a king or queen.

Sanctions Way of enforcing a decision – for example, by means of a trade boycott.

Satellite states Countries under the domination of a foreign power.

Secret Police Police agency which operates in secret to protect national security. Generally used to frighten opponents and critics of a government.

Senate The Upper House of the US Congress (parliament).

Six Day War of 1967 The war between Israel and its Arab neighbours which lasted six days in June 1967.

SLBM A submarine launched ballistic missile.

Sphere of influence Region of the world in which one state is dominant.

Strategic bomber(s) A large aircraft designed to drop large amounts of bombs on a distant target for the purposes of diminishing an enemy's capacity to wage war.

Strategic warheads Those warheads that are linked to their delivery vehicle and ready for launch.

Truman Doctrine US President Truman's idea that it was the USA's duty to prevent the spread of communism to eastern Europe and the rest of the world. To do this, he was also prepared to engage the USA in military enterprises all over the world.

United Nations The international body set up in 1945 to promote peace and international co-operation and security.

Vietnam War Usually given to be the conflict between the USA and North Vietnam and the Vietcong.

Warsaw Pact A military treaty and association, formed in 1955, of the Soviet Union and and its European satellite states.

Index

Afghanistan, Soviet invasion of 74, 75, 83, 84–6, 87, 106
Albania 72
Amin, Hafizullah 84–5
Andropov, Yuri 89, 92, 93
Apollo-Soyuz space mission 81
Arab-Israeli conflicts 45, 76, 79, 80
arms race 8, 18, 39, 40, 56, 98, 100
Attlee, Clement 17

Baltic states 105
Bay of Pigs invasion 58–9
Berlin
    Berlin airlift 33, 36–7
    Berlin Crisis (1948–49) 33–7
    Berlin Crisis (1961) 50–4
    Berlin Wall 49, 51–2, 53–4, 104, 105
Bolsheviks 10–11, 13
Brezhnev, Leonid 66, 68, 69, 76, 77, 78, 80, 81, 82, 83, 85, 89, 93
Brezhnev Doctrine 72, 76, 98, 104
brinkmanship 48
Bulgaria 16, 23, 25, 26, 103
Bush, George 97, 102

capitalism 10, 27, 41, 48, 66
Carter, Jimmy 83, 86, 87
Carter Doctrine 86
Castro, Fidel 57, 58, 59, 60
Ceausescu, Nicolai 72, 103
CFE (Conventional Armed Forces in Europe) Treaty 102
Chernenko, Konstantin 93, 94
China 40, 72, 77, 85, 93
Churchill, Winston 7, 11, 12, 13, 14, 15, 17, 21, 23, 25, 56
CIA (Central Intelligence Agency) 58, 59
Cold War
        Berlin Crisis (1948–49) 33–7
    Berlin Crisis (1961) 50–4
    blame for 18–19
    Cuban Missiles Crisis 48, 55, 57–63
    détente 55, 63, 65, 72, 75, 76–7, 83, 86, 87, 88, 94, 97
    duration 8
    early Cold War 21–30
    end of 74, 97, 98–106
    features 8
    Hungarian uprising 41, 43–6
    origins 7–19
    second Cold War 74, 83
collectivisation 26, 50
Comecon 26, 42
Cominform 25, 26, 28, 42
communism 10, 23, 24, 25, 26, 27, 28, 40, 41, 42, 60, 66, 68, 72, 76
    anti-communism 7, 11, 28, 40, 48, 59, 88
containment policy 21, 27, 28, 38
Cruise and Pershing missiles 89, 90, 94
Cuban Missiles Crisis 48, 55, 57–63
Czechoslovakia 16, 25, 26, 65–72, 103
    Prague Spring 68–9
    Soviet invasion 69, 70–2, 76

détente 55, 63, 65, 72, 75, 76–7, 83, 86, 87, 88, 94, 97
domino theory 40
Dubcek, Alexander 66, 68, 69, 70, 71
Dulles, John Foster 44, 48

Eisenhower, Dwight 44, 50, 51, 56, 58

Geneva Accord 100
Germany
    East Germany 26, 35, 37, 49, 53, 103, 104–5
    reunification 103, 105
    West Germany 35, 37, 49, 53, 69, 82, 104–5
    see also Berlin
glasnost 98, 99
Gorbachev, Mikhail 94, 97, 98–9, 100, 101, 102, 104, 105, 106
'Gorbymania' 101
Greece 23, 27, 28
Gulf War, First 102

Helsinki Agreements 74, 75, 77, 82–3
Hitler, Adolf 11
human rights issues 75, 82, 83
Hungary 16, 22, 23, 25, 26, 41–6, 103, 104
    Hungarian uprising 41, 43–6
Hussein, Saddam 102

INF (Intermediate Nuclear Forces Treaty) 100, 101, 106
Iranian hostage crisis 86
Iron Curtain 21, 50, 51, 104
Islamic fundamentalism 85

Kadar, Janos 44, 45, 46
Kennedy, John F. 50, 51, 53, 55, 57, 58, 59, 61, 62, 63
Khrushchev, Nikita 40, 41, 42, 44, 46, 50–1, 53, 57, 60, 62, 63
Kissinger, Henry 82
Korean War 8, 40

Lenin, Vladimir 10
linkage policy 76, 78
loans and aid 8
    see also Marshall Plan

McCarthy, Joe 40
MAD (Mutually Assured Destruction) 8, 89
Mao Zedong 40, 44, 63
Marshall Plan 21, 26, 28–30, 34, 42
Masaryk, Jan 25, 66
Mindszenty, Cardinal 44
Monroe Doctrine 59

Nagy, Imre 25, 43, 44, 45
NATO (North Atlantic Treaty Organisation) 8, 33, 37, 38–9, 50, 56, 63, 68, 83, 105
Nazi-Soviet Pact 11
Nixon, Richard 76, 77, 78, 79, 80
Novotny, Antonin 66, 67
nuclear weapons 8, 17, 18, 27, 40, 50, 56, 63, 78, 80, 88, 89, 91, 92, 94, 101, 102
    see also arms race
NUTS (Nuclear Utilization Target Selection) 89, 94

Olympic Games boycotts 86, 93

Palach, Jan 71
percentages deal 23
perestroika 98, 99
Poland 11, 12, 13, 15, 16, 18, 22, 23, 24, 91, 103, 104
    Warsaw Uprising 13

Potsdam Conference 16–17
Prague Spring 68–9
propaganda 8

Rakosi, Matyas 42, 43
Reagan, Ronald 74, 87, 88, 89, 91, 92, 93, 100, 101, 106
Reykjavik Summit 101
Romania 16, 22, 23, 24, 26, 72, 103
Roosevelt, Franklin D. 7, 12, 14, 17, 25
Russian Civil War 10, 13

Sakharov, Andrei 83, 93
SALT I and II 63, 74, 75, 78, 80, 83, 86
SDI (Strategic Defence Initiative – Star Wars) 91, 92, 97, 100, 101
Second World War 6, 7, 9, 11, 12–17, 22, 42
Sinatra Doctrine 104
Six Day War 76
Solidarity 91
Soviet Union
    collapse of 103, 105
    de-Stalinisation 46, 66
    expansion 17, 18, 19, 21, 22–3, 25, 38
    reforms 98, 99
    satellite states 24–5, 46, 66, 98, 105
space exploration 8, 81
Sputnik 56
spying 8, 50
Stalin, Joseph 7, 11, 12, 13, 14, 15, 16, 17, 18, 23, 25, 28, 29, 34, 36, 39, 40
START (Strategic Arms Reduction Talks) 91, 102
Suez Canal 45
Svoboda, Ludvik 66–7

Teheran Conference 12–13
Tito, Marshal 25, 26, 69
Treaty of Versailles 17, 18
Truman, Harry 17, 18, 25, 28, 36, 37, 40
Truman Doctrine 26, 27–8, 50

U-2 spy planes 8, 50, 56, 60
United Nations 12, 14, 16, 44, 51, 102

Vietnam War 8, 72, 76, 77

Warsaw Pact 8, 33, 39, 44, 56, 68, 69, 72, 104, 105
Warsaw Uprising 13
weapons treaties 63, 65, 76, 78, 101, 102

Yalta Conference 14–15
Yeltsin, Boris 105
Yom Kippur War 79, 80
Yugoslavia 23, 25